SOURCEE

VISUAL IDEAS

MW01519242

SOURCEBOOK OF
VISUAL IDEAS

EDITED BY STEVEN HELLER & SEYMOUR CHWAST

VNR VAN NOSTRAND REINHOLD
New York

Acknowledgments

▌P Pushpin Editions

Producer: Steven Heller
Designer: Seymour Chwast
Assistant Editors: Hyland Baron
                  Debora Schuler
Associate Designer: Roxanne Slimak
Production: Jeff Powers

Project Manager: Julie Lasky

Printed in the United States of America

Van Nostrand Reinhold
115 Fifth Avenue
New York, New York 10003

Van Nostrand Reinhold International Company
Limited
11 New Fetter Lane
London EC4P 4EE, England

Van Nostrand Reinhold
480 La Trobe Street
Melbourne, Victoria 3000, Australia

Macmillan of Canada
Division of Canada Publishing Corporation
164 Commander Boulevard
Agincourt, Ontario M1S 3C7, Canada

16 15 14 13 12 11 10 9 8 7 6 5 4 3 2 1

**Library of Congress Cataloging-in-
Publication Data**

Heller, Steven.
  Sourcebook of visual ideas.

  Includes index.
  1. Communication in design. 2. Visual
perception. I. Chwast, Seymour. II. Title.
NK1510.H437 1989   745.4   88-20762
ISBN 0-442-23271-3

The authors' sincerest gratitude goes to Debbie
Schuler and Hyland Baron, who devoted long
hours of labor and unflagging energy to this project, and without whom this project would never
have happened. To Roxanne Slimak, who ex-
pertly juggled the design elements. To Jeff
Powers, who administered the production. To
Lilly Kaufman, our editor at Van Nostrand Reinhold, for her patience and support, and Julie
Lasky, our project manager at Van Nostrand
Reinhold. To Edward Spiro for additional photography. And to Sarah Jane Freymann, our
agent. We would also like to thank all art directors, designers, and illustrators who generously
contributed their time and material.

Contents

Introduction

The visual idea is the cornerstone of graphic design and illustration today. The practice even has a name: *conceptual illustration and design.* While once these forms primarily served the decorative needs of a printer, advertiser, or editor, today's illustrators and designers are called upon to clarify difficult intellectual, often abstract, problems. This is, in part, the result of the revolution in electronic media and information processing that fosters the rapid transmission of complex data. Although video and print address distinctly different communications needs, they are, nevertheless, in direct competition for viewer attention and comprehension. Even though the television image is fleeting and the printed word is static, it is necessary to employ alluring visual "signposts" simply to encourage someone to read. Therefore, illustration and graphic design have become integral adjuncts, not merely slaves, to text by offering readers various levels of intellectual and emotional experience. The range of information has also increased to include complex subject matter once deemed too difficult to illustrate.

The editorial illustrator is regularly commissioned to visualize, symbolize, and otherwise explain such current issues as technology, genetic engineering, and environmental decay and such abstract concepts as illness, ethics, and aging. Graphic designers are also responsible for making ideas and services as diverse as rape counseling, school registration, and real-estate investment accessible through posters, logos, advertisements, and brochures. For this, the practitioner must be a skilled interpreter and manipulator of words and pictures.

Simply defined, a visual idea is a pictorial response to an abstract problem that may be general (e.g., symbolize *peace)* or specific (e.g., describe *American oil dependency on foreign suppliers).* The visual idea should concisely present complex meanings that would otherwise take many words to explain. Visual ideas are developed by the manipulation, interpretation, and juxtaposition of familiar and not-so-familiar pictorial elements into an image or images that convey, either literally or figuratively, specific meaning. The most successful visual ideas are those double entendres or visual puns which attract the viewer by their pictorial, aesthetic, or even emotional merits yet impart a distinct message.

Visual ideas are conveyed in various ways. In illustration and graphic design, the most common method is that oft-denigrated form of wordplay, the pun, which, according to Eli Kince, author of *Visual Puns in Design,* has been given greater respect as a tool of visual language. The pun, Kince writes, results when "the viewer becomes aware that one or more symbols created two or more possible meanings or associations applicable in one context." This is practiced in typography, caricature, photography, and countless other graphic applications. A wonderful example is a Volkswagen advertisement in which the VW logo is etched onto an effervescent tablet resembling an Alka-Seltzer that is dissolving in water. The headline reads: "If gas pains persist, try Volkswagen." Even without reading the words, the viewer can make the quick association between the VW automobile and the idea of fast relief.

When the pun succeeds, the viewer is usually taken off

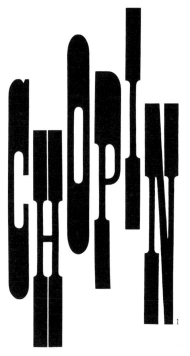

1. *Paul Rand, Westinghouse Electric Corp., 1971.*
2. *Peter Kuper, New York Times Book Review, Spring 1987 (special Mind, Body, Health issue). A.D.: Steven Heller.* 3. *Traditional.* 4. *Brad Holland, Art of The Times, 1973, A.D.: J. C. Suares.* 5. *Seymour Chwast, New York Times Magazine. A.D.: Ruth Ansel.* 6. *Gottfried Helnwein, see page 22.* 7. *Lou Dorfsman, CBS program ad, The New York Times.*

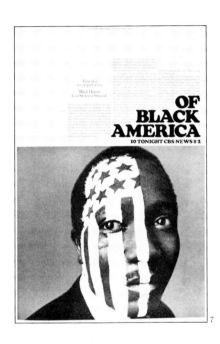

guard. There is often a similar effect on the creator as well, for, as Paul Rand writes in *Paul Rand: A Designer's Art,* the pun, or for that matter any humorous association, is often a fortuitous accident: "The development of any visual image must begin with some tangible idea, conscious or otherwise. It should come as no surprise that, more often than not, creative ideas are the product of chance, intuition, or accident, later justified to fit some prevailing popular theory, practical need, or formal obsession."

Alan Hurlburt adds in *The Design Concept* that "[o]ne of the most important sources of visual ideas is our accumulated perceptual experience—the visual record that is stored for future retrieval." Quite often a personal association is triggered by a text, brief, or problem provided by the client and then developed by the illustrator or designer. As an example, for a special insert to *The New York Times Book Review* devoted to books about mind, body, and health, Peter Kuper was asked to conceive a cover illustration that tied together these related ideas. Drawing on his love of children's book illustration, Kuper created an anthropomorphized tree that flexed its leafless, muscular limbs as if it were a bodybuilder. On the limbs were various birds, each representing a different aspect of the overall theme. Although one might interpret the metaphor as a tree of life, this would be only an after-the-fact justification for a basically intuitive response to the problem.

Other means of developing visual ideas are more intellectually motivated and involve deliberate use of symbolism, analogy, and metaphor.

A **symbol** is an image that is reduced to its essence, such as a flag, logo, or trademark. The Stars and Stripes evoke America; balanced scales suggest justice; a dove represents peace. The best symbolic solutions, however, need not be timeworn clichés or stereotypes such as Uncle Sams, dollar signs, or cornucopias. Many symbols are either reinterpreted or newly invented to suit modern definitions as they change with time and lose their effectiveness. For example, from the late 1800s to the very recent past, industrial smokestacks symbolized progress, while today they represent pollution. The wide-mouthed, nuclear steamstack, associated with Three Mile Island, suggests an even worse pox on the environment. At the turn of the century, the caricature of the fat, diamond-studded, tuxedo-clad gentleman represented the capitalist mogul; today, yuppie pinstripes and pastel ties are the symbols of preference. Indeed, running shoes and Walkmen have also replaced diamond studs as symbols of a new affluence. Some time-honored symbols have simply, and perhaps temporarily, lost their effectiveness because of overuse, while others will never be rendered ineffective. A skull and crossbones, for example, when used on a dangerous product, loudly screams "hazardous to your health."

With today's unrelenting image barrage, symbols are often misused and abused by illustrators and designers who are either disconnected from their subjects or irresponsibly trying new means of communicating old ideas. Yet new, effective images are indeed possible if a person has an inventive mind. And not all symbols need be dispassionately removed from the artist's experience. As Ben Shahn wisely warns in *The Shape of Content,* "in the abstracting of an idea one may lose the very intimate humanity of it." Hence, new symbols should emerge from the "marriage" of personal experience and universal knowledge. Two significant examples are by illustrators Robert Osborn and Brad Holland. Osborn invented an image of tremendous power: the mushroom cloud/human skull. In early 1946, only

Introduction

months after the first atomic bomb was dropped over Hiroshima, this cartoon became a poignant emblem of nuclear madness. In the early 1970s, responding to an assignment to illustrate America's impending oil shortage, Holland made an extraordinary graphic discovery. Rather than show the conventional gas pump or oil well being manipulated by a stereotypical Arab sheik, Holland recalled his (and our) all-but-forgotten grade-school knowledge of prehistory and fossil fuels, and he drew a tyrannosaurus rex flowing from an oil drum. In each case, the artist has touched responsive chords in viewers by transcending the obvious.

Analogy is another method for developing the visual idea in which two disparate elements are made similar. As an example, take a 1967 advertisement for Esso (now Exxon) gasoline with a headline that reads, ''Refuel Anywhere.'' It shows a photograph of a hummingbird feeding on a flower. The analogy rests on the idea that like a hummingbird, which can fill itself up on any flower, the motorist can replenish his gas supply virtually anywhere in the world with Esso gasoline. This is a perfect word-image analogy. A pure visual analogy is one in which the word-image relationship is not a requisite.

A visual **metaphor** is the logical substitution of one image for another, with the two images sometimes related only by common agreement. For example, the common vis-

ual metaphor for old age is an hourglass or watch face; for war, a knight or a sword; for love, a cupid or a heart. A good example of a somewhat less common but equally logical illustrative metaphor is a drawing for an article on self-testing for alcoholism. In it, Seymour Chwast has substituted a monkey for a man because the animal is a common subject of laboratory experiments. Through anthropomorphism, Chwast has imbued the monkey with characteristics appropriate to the research scientist; giving it a stethoscope, he has shown the monkey clearly conducting a self-test. This skewed image *forces* the viewer to ponder the ironic relationship. And it is not only an apt metaphor, but also a well-rendered and -composed artwork which successfully conveys its message. Without a talented maker, a good verbal idea can be a bad visual one. Moreover, a verbal metaphor does not always translate well into visual terms. Attempting to visualize something that is actually best conveyed in words can be an excruciating process that results in overworked art.

Visual ideas should identify, inform, and persuade, but they are not always neatly pigeonholed in the categories mentioned previously. A visual idea is not always a puzzle. It can be an absurd juxtaposition of elements in a collage or montage. For example, Gottfried Helnwein's cautionary message about nuclear war is based on an effective surreal

8. *Logos: William Golden, CBS; Lester Beall, International Paper; Rob Janoff, Apple Computer.* 9. *Milton Glaser, New York Magazine.* 10. *Robert Grossman, The Atlantic Monthly.* 11. *Herb Lubalin, American Institute of Graphic Arts poster exhibition.* 12. *Woody Pirtle, Aubrey Hair trademark, 1973.* 13. *James Miho, see page 140.*

relationship that owes its strength to its stark realism; as pictured, a nuclear warhead is about equal to the size of an adult head. Another striking juxtaposition is shown in Lou Dorfsman's full-page newspaper advertisement promoting a television documentary about being black in America. In it, half of a black man's face is painted white with the Stars and Stripes. It is an ironic statement, but more important, it is completely unexpected. Moreover, it not only serves as a persuasive hook for the series, it transcends its immediate function by becoming an icon of the American black experience.

A visual idea can also be a graphic exclamation point. Many trademarks, such as those for CBS, International Paper, and Apple Computer, are not so totally abstracted, as is the current trend in trademarks, that they are not also recognizable as ideas. The first image is a quintessential television one; the second, a schematic of a tree; and the third, a revitalized fruit of knowledge.

A visual idea, however, need not be a single image. Serial illustrations can be equally effective. Milton Glaser's four pieces done for *New York* magazine which depict drug addiction are poetic, yet strident, commentaries. Robert Grossman's visual "essay" in *The Atlantic* magazine about protecting America from nuclear attack is an acerbic satire on the recent "star wars" policy.

Most visual ideas are transmitted through illustration (a painting, a drawing, or a photograph) wed to words, but illustration is not the only vehicle. Herb Lubalin was a master at expressing meaning through typographical images, whereby a headline or other type treatment *was* the illustra-

tion. Lubalin's antiwar poster, which reads, "The Next War Will Not Determine What Is Right But What Is Left," presents the type as not only an ironic verbal statement, but, by including photographs of cockroaches in the word *Left*, a total *picture*. Less acerbic, but just as clever, Woody Pirtle's "Hair" logo shows a logical, yet surprising, marriage of word and image.

Impressionistic or expressionistic renderings are not necessarily visual ideas, but that does not mean that a visual idea cannot be rendered in an impressionistic or expressionistic manner. In fact, many striking ideas result because a design style dominates. For example, James Miho's poster for the Smithsonian Institution Traveling Service is decidedly his impression of the future, in which the visual components, though recognizably futuristic, are not tied together by overt symbolism but by the designer's aesthetics and taste. Miho's poster imparts a specific message and creates an environment or mood.

Sourcebook of Visual Ideas is a compilation of some of the most successful conceptual illustrations and designs made during the past ten years, a unique compendium of interesting solutions to very common recurring themes and subjects. The material was chosen from scores of designer and illustrator annuals, exhibitions, newspapers, and magazines. It is not intended to show you *how* to create visual ideas or to serve as a clip file; rather, it will provide models, showing how others have solved common problems in fresh ways, while underscoring how personal style increases the effectiveness of an idea.

—STEVEN HELLER

10

11

12

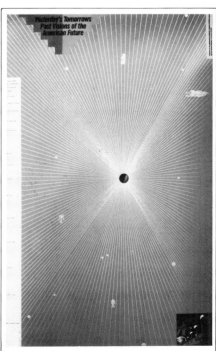

13

Aging

Elderly, Old, Venerable, Ancient, Mature

Stereotypes of aging, often demeaning and untrue, are prevalent in popular imagery. Symbols of age such as clocks, hourglasses, setting suns, and falling leaves suggest passage of life.

Problem: Depict the concept "Sequences" for a paper promotional campaign.
Artist: Dugald Stermer
Art Director: Jim Cross
Designer: Dugald Stermer
Client: Simpson Paper Company

Problem: Illustrate an article on the problem of dependent elderly parents.
Artist: Dugald Stermer
Art Director: Dugald Stermer
Publication: California Living (the Sunday magazine of the *San Francisco Examiner & Chronicle*)

Problem: Illustrate an article entitled "Frank of Oregon."
Artist: Marshall Arisman
Art Director: Robert Priest
Designer: Judy Goldstein
Publication: Esquire

Problem: Depict the rapid passage of a lifetime.
Artist: Charles B. Slackman
Art Director: Rhoda Gubernick
Publication: The Atlantic

Animals

Wildlife, Fauna, Beasts, Men, Creatures

Animals in satiric art date back to early Egyptian papyrus in which anthropomorphized creatures represent the folly and foibles of human beings. Animals are still used for such purposes.

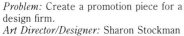

Problem: Create a promotion piece for a design firm.
Art Director/Designer: Sharon Stockman
Client: North Charles Street Design Organization

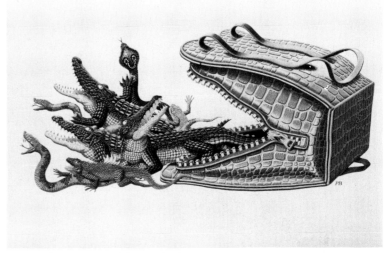

Problem: Illustrate an article on animals whose existence is endangered by the fashion industry.
Artist: Peter Brookes
Art Director: Michael Rand
Publication: The Sunday Times Magazine, London

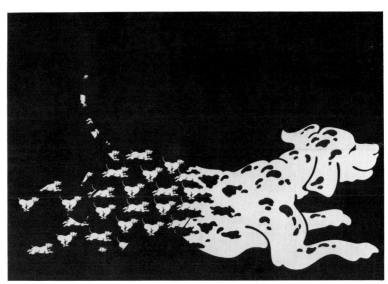

Problem: Design and illustrate a moving announcement.
Art Director: Martin Bennett
Designer: Randall Hensley
Client: North Charles Street Design Organization

Animals

Problem: Illustrate a poster promoting a
film festival.
Artist: Alex Murawski
Art Director: David Bartels
Client: Bruce Bendinger

Problem: Design a ''Past Due'' stamp
for accounting department use.
Artist: Harrison Saunders
Art Director: Mike Hicks
Client: Hixo, Inc.

Problem: Design a traffic-control stamp
for interoffice use.
Artist: Harrison Saunders
Art Director: Mike Hicks
Client: Hixo, Inc.

Problem: Design an engaging package for
a pet odor-removal product.
Artist: Cap Pannell
Art Directors: Cap Pannell and Carol St. George
Client: NCH Corporation

LEONARD J. WAXDECK'S
BIRD CALLING CONTEST

MAY 16, 1985 THE THEATRE PIEDMONT HS

DALLAS ZOO

Problem: Design a logo for a zoo.
Artist: Dick Mitchell
Art Director: Dick Mitchell
Client: The Dallas Zoo

Problem: Design a logo for a humane society.
Artist: Luis D. Acevedo
Art Director: Luis D. Acevedo
Client: Lewisville Humane Society

Problem: Illustrate a poster for a bird-calling competition.
Artist: Alex Murawski
Art Director: David Bartels
Client: Leonard J. Waxdeck

13

Animals

Problem: Design promotional signage for a zoo.
Artist: Lance Wyman
Art Directors: Lance Wyman and Bill Cannan
Client: National Zoological Park, Smithsonian Institution

Problem: Illustrate an editorial on mating animals in captivity.
Artist: Devis Grebu
Art Director: Jerelle Kraus
Publication: The New York Times

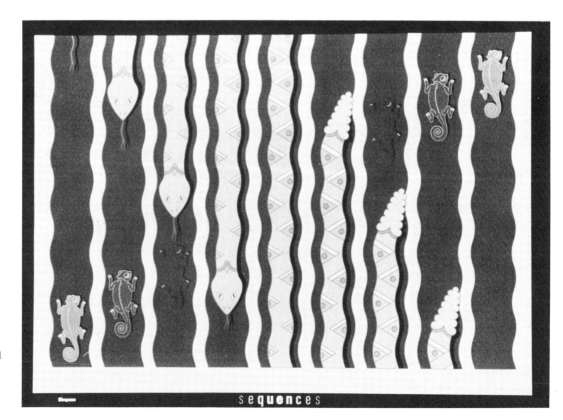

Problem: Create a promotional poster for a paper company.
Artist: Rex Peteet
Art Director: James Cross
Client: Simpson Paper Co.

Art

Masterpiece, Classic, Painting, Pièce de Résistance, Genius, Depiction (See Crafts, Dance, Fashion, Film, Theatre)

The tools of art provide its primary symbols; the brush, palette, paint tube, and canvas are the common clichés. Yet as art transcends the ordinary, the representation of art should do so too.

Problem: Create a cover illustration for *Time* magazine.
Artist: Eugene Mihaesco
Art Director: Walter Bernard
Publication: Time

Problem: Design a call-for-entries poster for the AIGA Package Design competition.
Art Director: Roger Cook
Designer: Don Shanosky
Client: American Institute of Graphic Arts

The Tyler Offset Workshop

Problem: Design a poster showcasing black-and-white and color reproduction techniques.
Artist: George Tscherny
Art Director: George Tscherny
Client: Tyler Offset Workshop

Problem: Create a symbol/mark for a graphic design studio.
Artist: Larry Brekke
Designer: Mike Bruner
Client: Graphic Traffic Art Studio, Bismarck, ND

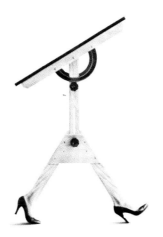

Problem: Create a logo/symbol for an artists' representative.
Art Director/Designer: Sue T. Crolick
Client: Sandra Heinen, Inc.

Art

Problem: Design a poster for an
exhibition of American paintings from the
Metropolitan Museum of Art
Artist: Louis Danziger
Art Director: Louis Danziger
Client: Los Angeles County Museum of Art

Problem: Illustrate "designer's block"
(drawing a blank) for a trade magazine
cover.
Artist: Elwood H. Smith
Art Director: Yoshihisa Ishihara
Client: Idea

Problem: Create a cover illustration for
The Boston Globe Magazine issue
promoting its annual photo contest.
Artist: Steven Guarnaccia
Art Director: Lynn Staley
Publication: The Boston Globe Magazine

Problem: Create a cover illustration for
an issue of *Print* magazine.
Artist: Philippe Weisbecker
Art Director: Charlie Hess
Publication: Print

Problem: Design a poster to promote the Museum of Neon Art.
Artist: Lili Lakich
Art Directors: Phillip Ross and Lynn Beda
Client: Jannes Art Publishing

Problem: Design a self-portrait poster to promote an exhibition of one's own work.
Artist: Beat Brüsch
Art Director: Beat Brüsch
Client: Centre Culturel Régional Delémont

Problem: Design a promotional mailer for a photographer.
Artist: Patrick Coyne
Art Director: Patrick Coyne
Client: Charly Franklin Photography

Problem: Design a poster promoting a printer.
Artist: John Muller
Art Director: John Muller
Client: Solna Printing

Art

Problem: Design a poster promoting a student creative competition.
Artist: Dick Mitchell
Art Director: Dick Mitchell
Client: Dallas Society of Visual Communicators

Problem: Design a cover for a trade magazine feature on the American Institute of Architects meeting in Dallas.
Artist: Tony Palladino
Art Director: Tony Palladino
Publication: Architectural & Engineering News

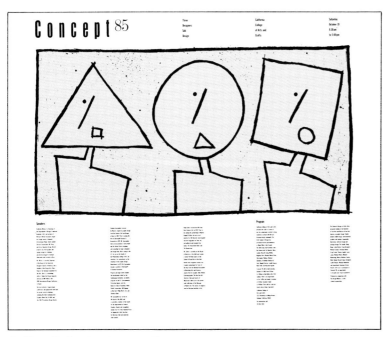

Problem: Design a poster promoting an evening of speakers on design.
Artist: Michael Mabry
Art Director: Michael Mabry
Client: California College of Arts and Crafts

Problem: Design an announcement for an exhibition of paintings and textiles.
Artist: Bob Cosgrove
Art Director: Bob Cosgrove
Clients: Bob and Marge Cosgrove and Studio San Guiseppe

Atomic

Nuclear, Minute, Particle, Armageddon, Elemental, (See Bomb, Energy, Politics, Power, and War)

Since the bomb was dropped over Hiroshima, the mushroom cloud has been the specter of doom. Conversely, the image of a nucleus with orbiting electrons suggests the optimistic uses of nuclear energy.

Problem: Create a cover illustration for a feature article on the hazards of nuclear power.
Artist: Marshall Arisman
Art Director: Rudy Hoglund
Publication: Time

Problem: Create an illustration depicting the danger of irradiated foods.
Artist: Ken Rinciari
Editor: Colin Penno
Client: The Messenger, Santa Monica Mountain News & Arts Publication

Problem: Depict the lack of world cognizance of the responsibilities of the atomic age.
Artist: Bob Fortier
Art Director: Bob Fortier
Client: Unpublished

Atomic

Problem: Create an ironic illustration for an article on American war paranoia.
Artist: Andrzej Dudzinski
Art Director: Ronn Campisi
Publication: The Boston Globe

Problem: Illustrate a naive article on post-apocalyptic life.
Artist: Anita Kunz
Art Director: Kent Barton
Publication: Sunshine magazine, Ft. Lauderdale

Birth

All cultures have common images for fertility and conception. In most, spring suggests awakening or beginning, yet, strangely, in our industrialized society the stork is the most common representation of birth.

Problem: Design an invitation to a baby shower.
Artist: Chris Rovillo
Art Director: Chris Rovillo
Client: The Rouse Company

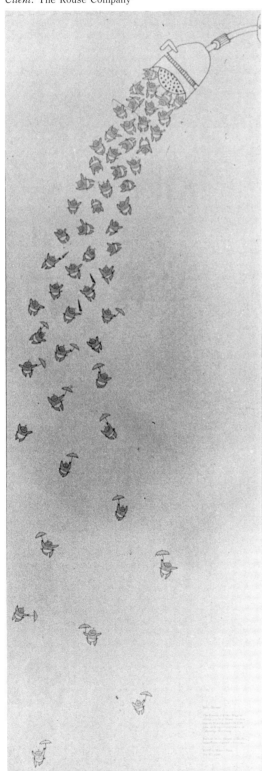

Problem: Design a birth announcement for Susan Leigh Wylie.
Artist: Mervil M. Paylor
Art Director: Mervil M. Paylor
Clients: Ed and Lou Wylie (parents)

Problem: Design a poster to arouse interest in birth control.
Artist: Giancarlo Iliprandi
Art Director: Giancarlo Iliprandi
Client: AIED (Italian Association for Demographic Education)

Bomb

A-Bomb, H-Bomb, Armageddon,
Nuclear, Destruction, Blitz, Holocaust
(See Atomic, Death, Energy, Politics,
and War)

In the eighteenth century a bomb was the shape of a basketball; by the turn of the nineteenth century the conical shape was developed. With the advent of air war, fins were added to the horrific toy. The mushroom cloud is now the primary specter.

Problem: Illustrate the nature of the superpowers' coexistence.
Artist: Horacio Fidel Cardo
Art Director: Jerelle Kraus
Publication: The New York Times

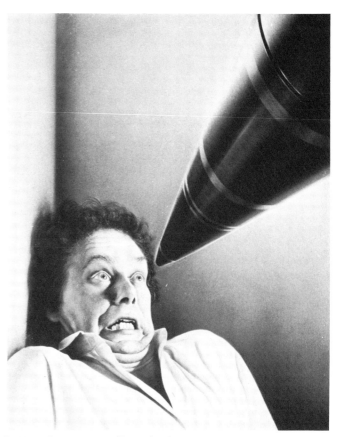

Problem: Create a cover illustration for a feature on fear of nuclear war.
Artist: Gottfried Helnwein
Art Director: Unknown
Publication: Der Spiegel

Problem: Illustrate an article on American attempts to make NATO defense missiles acceptable to Germany.
Artist: Henrik Drescher
Art Director: John McLeod
Designer: Lynn Staley
Client: INX News Graphics, Inc. (United Feature Syndicate)

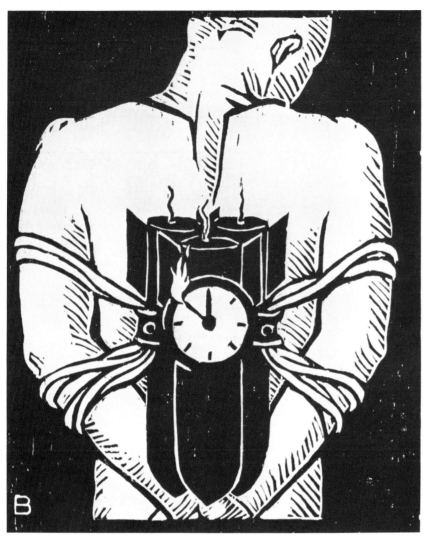

Problem: Create art for an antinuclear
book project.
Artist: Bascove
Art Director: Steven Heller
Client: Artists for Nuclear Freeze

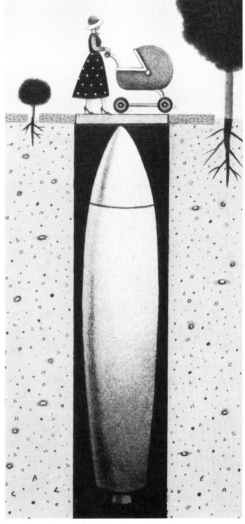

Problem: Create an illustration depicting
the public's lack of awareness regarding
the nuclear state of affairs.
Artist: Dave Calver
Art Director: Ken Kleppert
Publication: Psychology Today

Problem: Illustrate the attitude of West
Germans awaiting Pershings and cruise
missiles to be installed at NATO bases in
their country in the summer of 1983.
Artist: Hans Georg Rauch
Art Director: Jerelle Kraus
Publication: The New York Times

Problem: Create a cover illustration for
an article on European-American nuclear
defense relations.
Artist: Marshall Arisman
Art Director: Victor Navasky
Publication: The Nation

Bomb

Problem: Illustrate an article on the lack of communication in arms talks.
Artist: David Shannon
Art Director: John McLeod
Client: INX News Graphics, Inc. (United Feature Syndicate)

Problem: Depict awareness of the bomb as a pervasive element of American society.
Artist: Brad Holland
Art Director: John Twohey
Publication: The Chicago Tribune

Problem: Depict public disinterest in the nuclear freeze campaign.
Artist: Jacqueline Chwast
Art Director: Patrick J. B. Flynn
Publication: The Progressive

Business

Elegant top hats and diamond studs once represented the business tycoon, or "fat cat." Then, as now, class stratification was endemic to the stereotype. Yet today's white collar is a more common, if mundane, image.

Problem: Interpret "Accounting" for an idea book.
Artist: George Tscherny
Art Directors: Thomas Geismar and George Tscherny
Client: Xerox Corporation "Idea Book" series

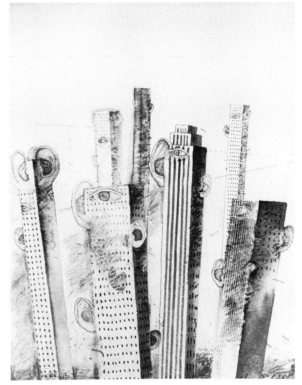

Problem: Illustrate an in-house magazine article on how corporations monitor one anothers' activities.
Artist: Alan Cober
Art Director: Peter Deutsch
Designer: Mark Ulrich
Client: AT&T

Problem: Illustrate an article on choosing a structure for your new business.
Artist: John Segal
Art Director: Richard Yeend
Publication: The New York Times

Problem: Illustrate an article on being trapped in a middle-management position.
Artist: Jerzy Kolacz
Art Director: Steve Manley
Publication: Canadian Business

Business

Problem: Design a cover for a book
exposing Coca-Cola Corporation politics.
Artist: Marc J. Cohen
Art Director: Bob Alucino
Client: Random House

Problem: Illustrate an article on how
business expansion is changing the
American life-style.
Artist: Seymour Chwast
Art Director: Judy Garlan
Publication: The Atlantic

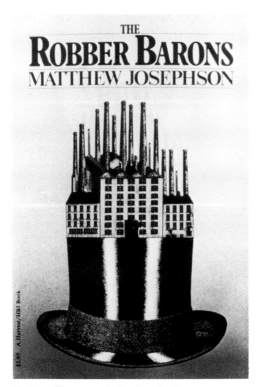

Problem: Illustrate a jacket for a book on
capitalism.
Artist: Richard Mantel
Art Director: Harris Lewine
Designer: Richard Mantel
Client: Harcourt Brace Jovanovich

Problem: Illustrate an editorial on
disbursement of funds intended for the
Nicaraguan *contras.*
Artist: Horacio Fidel Cardo
Art Director: Jerelle Kraus
Publication: The New York Times

Problem: Illustrate an article on
government deregulation of health and
safety protections.
Artist: Brad Holland
Art Director: Roger Black
Designer: Ken Kendrick
Publication: The New York Times
Magazine

Problem: Illustrate a newspaper article
on the new trend in etiquette courses for
business entertaining.
Artist: Bonnie Timmons
Art Director: Bonnie Timmons
Publication: The Denver Post

Problem: Design a poster promoting a
talk on retail marketplace signage.
Art Director: Harry Murphy
Designers: Harry Murphy and John
Gaccione
Client: San Francisco Society of
Communicating Arts

Problem: Illustrate an article on the
increasing use of RICO statutes in tax-
evasion prosecutions.
Artist: Charles B. Slackman
Art Director: Rhonda Kass
Publication: Forbes

Problem: Design a symbol for a civic
organization.
Designers: Don Weller, Dennis Juett, and
Chikako Matsubayashi
Client: Los Angeles Junior Chamber of
Commerce

Celebration

Commemoration, Party, Observance, Ritual, Ceremony, Amusement, Blowout, Happening (See Birth, Christmas, Dance, Flag, and Peace)

Confetti, banners, and fireworks are the traditional means of celebrating an event. Graphically interpreted, they are also stylistic tools used to salute and make merry.

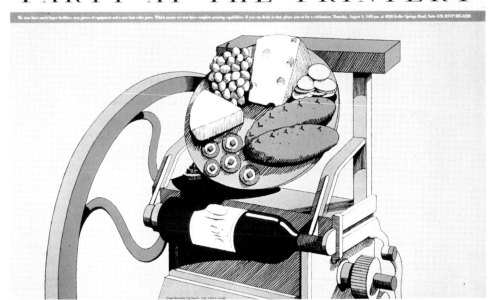

Problem: Design a poster for a celebration held at a printing plant.
Art Director: Cap Pannell
Designer: Cap Pannell
Client: The Printery

Problem: Design a poster for an exhibition of student work on the theme of Halley's comet "sightings."
Artist: Jose Ortega
Art Directors: Bill Kobasz and Richard Wilde
Designers: Bill Kobasz and Robin Gilmore-Barnes
Client: School of Visual Arts

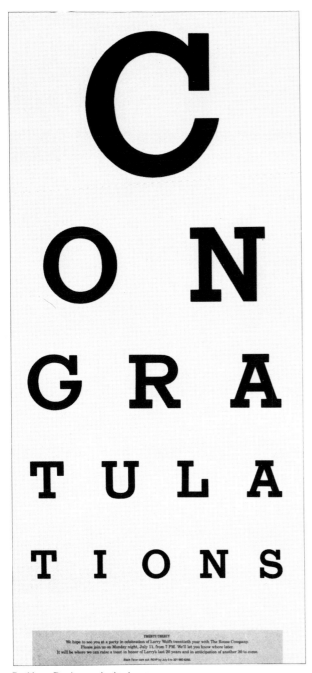

Problem: Design an invitation to a
company celebration.
Artist: Chris Rovillo
Art Director: Chris Rovillo
Client: The Rouse Company

Problem: Design a symbol for a class
reunion.
Artist: Mark Galarneau
Art Director: Mark Galarneau
Client: Blackford High School Class of 1977

Problem: Design an invitation for a party
at a construction firm.
Artist: Mike Schroeder
Art Director: Woody Pirtle
Designers: Woody Pirtle and
Mike Schroeder
Client: Gerald D. Hines Interests

Childhood

Youth, Salad Days, Infantilism, Immaturity, Babyhood, Naiveté, Juvenility (See Birth)

Youth connotes innocence, for which the lamb is the traditional symbol. Other symbols are the impish Pan or Puck. In contrast to the symbols for aging, symbols for youth express celebration of the world made new.

Problem: Illustrate an article on the embarrassment suffered by a gay child.
Artist: Bonnie Timmons
Art Director: David Miller
Designer: Gayle Sims
Publication: The Denver Post

Problem: Illustrate an article on the dangers and pitfalls facing children growing into adolescence.
Artist: Carolyn Gowdy
Art Director: Sue Costen
Client: Home and Law Magazines, Ltd.

Problem: Illustrate a story about the
growth of the paralegal profession.
Artist: Jim Jacobs
Art Director: Jim Jacobs
Publication: Legal Assistant Today

Problem: Illustrate "child prodigies."
Artist: Ken Rinciari
Art Director: Robert Best
Publication: New York

Problem: Design a symbol to convey the
essence of Japanese childhood.
Artist: Shigeo Fukuda
Art Director: Shigeo Fukuda
Client: Graphic Design Co., Ltd.

Christmas

No other Western holiday prompts such a plethora of symbolic representation. And no religious or secular image compares in ubiquitousness with Thomas Nast's classic Santa Claus.

Problem: Design a self-promotional Christmas card.
Artist: Anita Kunz
Art Director: Anita Kunz
Client: Anita Kunz

Problem: Design a magazine cover to run on Christmas day.
Artist: Patrick Blackwell
Art Director: Ronn Campisi
Publication: The Boston Globe Magazine

Problem: Design a Christmas card.
Artist: Hal Maythorpe
Art Director: Hal Maythorpe
Client: Unknown

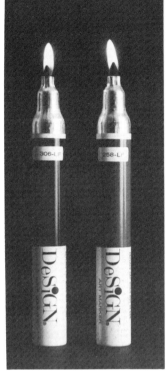

Problem: Design a Christmas card for an
advertising and design firm.
Photographer: Rod Pierce
Art Director: Sue T. Crolick
Designer: Sue T. Crolick
Client: Sue T. Crolick Advertising & Design

Problem: Design a self-promotional
Christmas card.
Photographer: John Dyer
Art Director: Roger Christian
Client: Roger Christian & Co., Inc.

Problem: Create an illustration on the
commercialization of Christmas.
Artist: Stuart Goldenberg
Art Director: Patrick J. B. Flynn
Publication: The Progressive

Problem: Design a Christmas card for an
advertising agency.
Artist: James Marsh
Art Director: Brian Morrow
Client: TBWA Advertising

Christmas

Problem: Illustrate an article on the psychology of gift giving.
Artist: Sandra Hendler
Art Director: Ken Newbaker
Publication: Philadelphia

Problem: Design a self-promotional Christmas card.
Art Director: Don Crum
Designers: Don Crum and Amy Werfel
Client: Don Crum & Co.

Problem: Design a Christmas card for an architect.
Artist: Sarah Lavicka
Art Director: Sarah Lavicka
Client: Holabird & Root/Architects

         Seasons Greetings! Holabird & Root

Computers

Data-processing, Word-processing, Ciphers, Calculators, Artificial Intelligence (See Business, Industry, Technology)

One of the most recurrent symbols of the late twentieth century, the computer consolidates two of the foremost images of the future past—the television and typewriter—into an icon of the age.

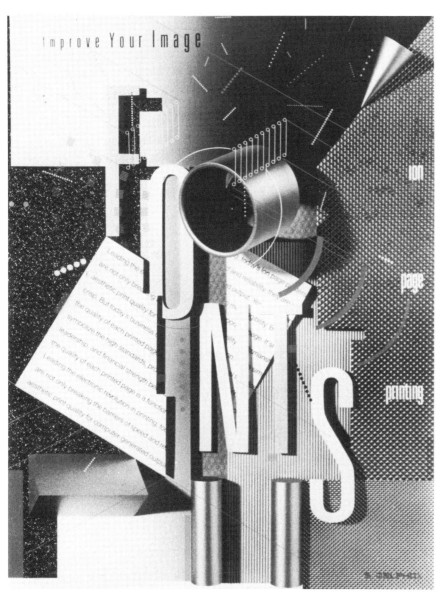

Problem: Design a poster promoting computer typography fonts.
Photographer: Tom Wedell
Art Director: Nancy Skolos
Client: Delphax Systems

Problem: Design a symbol for a firm that specializes in computer-generated comps for ad agencies.
Art Director: Dan O'Mara
Designers: Dan O'Mara, Jim Kellogg, and Wil Conerly
Client: Digital Art, Inc.

Problem: Design an identity and stationery system for a firm that trains and troubleshoots for first-time computer users.
Art Directors: Tom Cheevers and Pat O'Dell
Designers: Tom Cheevers and Pat O'Dell
Client: Computer Relief Services

Problem: Illustrate an article on individual privacy and personal information accessible to computers.
Artist: George Hardie
Art Director: David Hillman
Publication: Information Resource

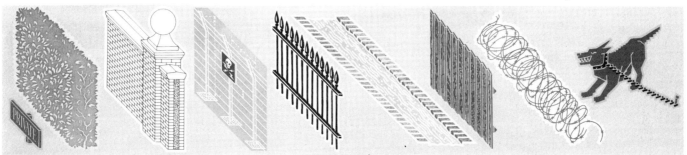

Computers

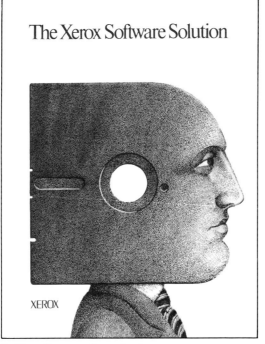

The Xerox Software Solution

XEROX

Problem: Create an illustration for a brochure promoting Xerox software products.
Artist: Jim Jacobs
Art Director: Al Weintraub
Client: Xerox Corporation

Problem: Illustrate an article on the role of the computer in the insurance business.
Artist: Rafal Olbinski
Art Director: Jim Hutch
Client: The Continental Insurance Company

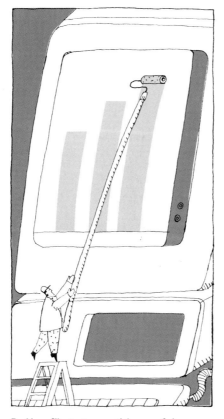

Problem: Illustrate an article on refining computer graphics programs.
Artist: John Segal
Art Director: Nancy Sterngold
Publication: The New York Times

Problem: Illustrate a story on computers in the workplace.
Artist: Philippe Weisbecker
Art Director: Nancy Rice
Publication: Byte

Crafts

Even in the computer age, handiwork remains endemic to cultural and business activity. Despite automation and robotics, materials produced by the individual are symbolic of past and present.

DESIGNED AND MADE FOR USE

Problem: Design a call for entries for a juried show of interior designs.
Art Director: John Waters
Client: American Craft Museum

Problem: Design a logo for a firm that specializes in custom-made cabinets.
Art Director: D. C. Stipp
Designer: D. C. Stipp
Client: Cabinetree

CABINETREE

Problem: Design a logo for the Dallas Handweavers and Spinners Guild.
Artist: Woody Pirtle
Art Director: Don Grimes
Designers: Don Grimes and Woody Pirtle
Client: Dallas Handweavers and Spinners Guild

Problem: Design a symbol for a potters' association.
Art Director: Felipe Taborda
Client: Ace-Rio Association, Rio de Janiero

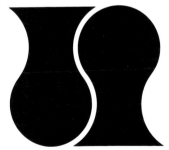

Problem: Design a trademark for a pottery maker.
Art Director: Félix Beltrán
Designer: Félix Beltrán
Client: Salles, Havana

Crime

The penal system provides a wealth of appropriate, if not comic, symbols, from the ball and chain to striped suits. But crime in the eighties is not so simple to depict. White-collar and victimless crimes require a broadened lexicon.

Problem: Illustrate a fiction piece on crime.
Artist: Douglas Fraser
Art Director: Deborah Rust
Publication: Harper's

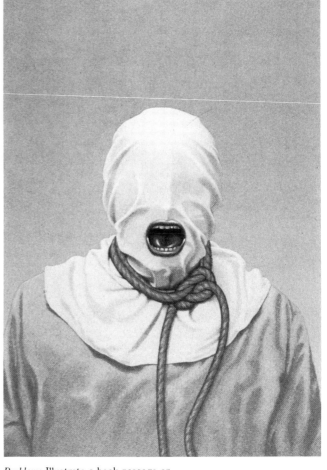

Problem: Illustrate a book passage on violence.
Artist: Henri Galeron
Art Director: Annie Galeron
Client: Okapi–Le Centurion

Problem: Illustrate an article on organized crime and labor unions in America.
Artist: Randall Enos
Art Director: Amy Willentz
Publication: The Nation

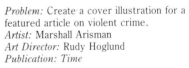

Dance

The varied rhythmic and discordant ges-
tures of dance multiply the number of representations of this art, which also
symbolizes the rites of all human activity.
Dance is at once ritualistic, suggesting
order, and formless, suggesting anarchy.

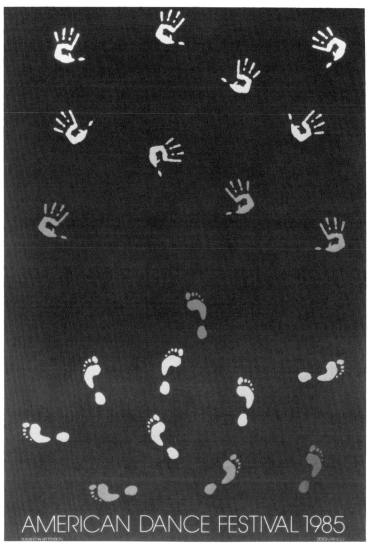

Problem: Design a poster that
depicts dance as both a modern
and ancient art.
Artist: Per Arnoldi
Art Director: Per Arnoldi
Client: American Dance Festival

Problem: Illustrate a short story
about an erotic cabaret in Paris.
Artist: George Snow
Art Director: Manuel Ortiz
Publication: Playboy

The Phoenix Club where the good times roll 7 p.m. through 2 a.m. daily, 5 p.m. through 2 a.m. Fridays and Saturdays. SUNDAY – Free Nachos and Draught Beer from 8 p.m. until it's gone. Bar Drinks and Beer $1.00 all night. MONDAY – Double Shot Night, 2 for 1 bar drinks all night. TUESDAY – Ladies' Night with 25¢ bar drinks. KSET Party first Tuesday of each month. WEDNESDAY – Bar Drinks and Draught Beer 50¢ from 7 p.m. to 11 p.m. Dance Contest with winners receiving $50 cash, $25 bar tab, and free event tickets. THURSDAY – Ladies' Night with 50¢ bar drinks from 7 p.m. to 11 p.m. FRIDAY – Free Bar-B-Q buffet and 2 for 1 bar drinks from 5 p.m. to 7 p.m. 1461 Lee Trevino at Trevino Plaza. Call 598-6545 for more information.

The club that Rocks El Paso. 1461 Lee Trevino.

Problem: Design a newspaper ad for a Texas rock-n-roll nightclub.
Artist: Bradford Lewton
Art Director: Roger Christian
Client: The Phoenix Club

Problem: Design a poster for a production of *The Nutcracker*.
Artist: Dan Bittman
Art Director: Dan Bittman
Client: Cincinnati Ballet Company

Problem: Design a cover for an album of break-dancing music.
Artist: Felipe Taborda
Art Director: Felipe Taborda
Client: Opus/Columbia Records

Death

Mortality, Demise, End, Decease, Extinction, Grim Reaper, Termination, Cessation of Life (See Aging, Birth, Drugs, War)

In Mexico, the Day of the Dead is joyfully celebrated as a time of resurrection with a panoply of comical skeleton masks and toys. The same images in other countries are frightening reminders of the final reward.

Problem: Illustrate an article entitled "The Bomb and Beyond."
Artist: Kathleen Calderwood
Art Director: Kerig Pope
Publication: Playboy

Problem: Illustrate an article entitled "Ghost Hunting."
Artist: Alexa Grace
Art Directors: Yolanda Como, Charles Churchward, and Shirley Lee
Designer: Charles Churchward
Publication: Vanity Fair

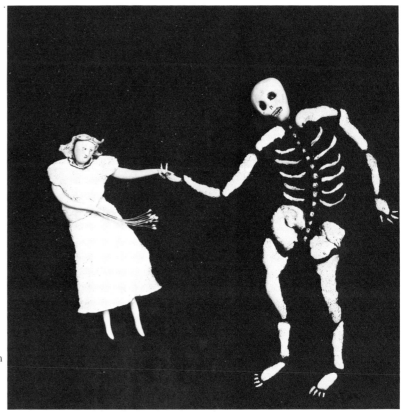

Problem: Create an illustration for use on an album cover.
Artist: Alexa Grace
Art Director: Christopher Austopchuk
Client: CBS Records

Drugs

Controlled Substances, Elixirs, Pharmaceuticals, Medicine, Treatment, Narcotics, Dope, Mickey Finns, Sedatives, Anaesthetics, Opiates (See Death, Medicine)

The use and abuse of prescription and illegal drugs is the subject of countless published reports. The capsule, hypodermic needle, and cocaine spoon are the most frequently used graphic reminders of drug use.

Problem: Illustrate an article on cocaine and Aspen, Colorado.
Artist: Tom Curry
Art Director: Greg Paul
Publication: The Plain Dealer

Problem: Depict the problem of coping with alcoholism.
Artist: Dagmar Frinta
Art Director: Ronn Campisi
Publication: The Boston Globe

The party begins.

I can drive when I drink.

2 drinks later

I can drive when I drink

After 4 drinks.

I can drive when I drink.

After 5 drinks.

I can drin when I driv

7 drinks in all.

I can drvrcdkrdrsz

The more you drink, the more coordination you lose. That's a fact, plain and simple.
Still, people drink too much and then go out and expect to handle a car.
When you drink too much you can't handle a car. You can't even handle a pen.

Seagram/distillers since 1857.

For enlarged reprints write Advertising Dept. F, Seagram Distillers Co., 375 Park Ave., N.Y., N.Y. 10022.

Problem: Create an illustration for an advertisement cautioning against drinking and driving.
Artist: Chuck Kintzing
Art Director: Chuck Kintzing
Designers: Chuck Kintzing and Dan Abramson
Client: Seagram Distillers

Problem: Create a poster illustration for an antidrug campaign.
Artist: Rafal Olbinski
Art Director: Rafal Olbinski
Client: Daytop

Economy

Business Climate, Stock Market, Management Trade (See Business, Industry)

Money is the fuel of economy and the subject of many graphic representations. But as complex as the various world economies have become, so are the images that symbolize the distribution of wealth.

Problem: Illustrate an article on Japan as America's major competitor for world economic superiority.
Artist: Eugene Mihaesco
Art Director: Robert Best
Publication: New York

Problem: Illustrate an article on the international stock market.
Artist: Rafal Olbinski
Art Director: Ken Serabian
Publication: Datamation

Problem: Illustrate an article on the gold standard.
Artist: Brad Holland
Art Director: Joan Hoffman
Publication: Fortune (illustration not used)

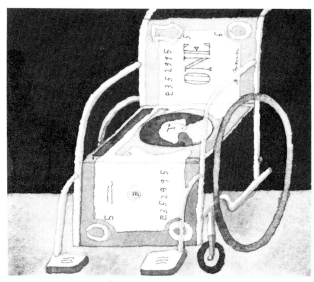

Problem: Illustrate an article on the cost of disability policies.
Artist: John Segal
Art Director: Mike Todd
Publication: The New York Times

Problem: Illustrate a news story on the effect of tax reform laws on the insurance business.
Artist: John Green
Art Director: Stan Huen
Publication: Dallas Times Herald

Problem: Create a cover illustration for a magazine serving the graphic design community.
Artist: Michael Mescall
Art Directors: Andrew Kner and James Cross
Designer: Michael Mescall
Publication: Print

Problem: Create a cover illustration for a feature story on the manufacturing and service sectors of the U.S. economy.
Artist: Kinuko Craft
Art Director: Everett Halvorsen
Designers: Roger Zapke and Rhonda Kass
Publication: Forbes

Problem: Illustrate an article urging the United States not to attempt to be at the forefront of the world economy.
Artist: John Craig
Art Director: Judy Garlan
Publication: The Atlantic

Problem: Create a chart to reflect the steep rise in oil prices.
Artist: Nigel Holmes
Art Director: Nigel Holmes
Publication: Time

Economy

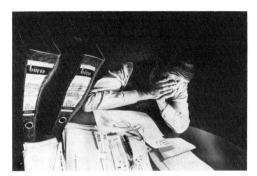

Problem: Depict the trauma of
bankruptcy
Artist: Jorg Hüber
Art Director: Ernest Pavlovic
Publication: Trend magazine, Austria

Problem: Illustrate an article on the
overwhelming array of choices facing
personal investors.
Artist: James Tughan
Art Director: Jackie Young
Designer: James Tughan
Publication: Financial Post

Problem: Illustrate a review of a book on
David Sarnoff and the future of the
communications industry.
Artist: Mirko Ilic
Art Director: Steven Heller
*Publication: The New York Times Book
Review*

Problem: Design small newspaper ads
that will promote a maximum number of
bank services yet be quickly legible.
Art Director: Marty Neumeier
Designer: Byron Glaser
Client: Santa Barbara Bank & Trust

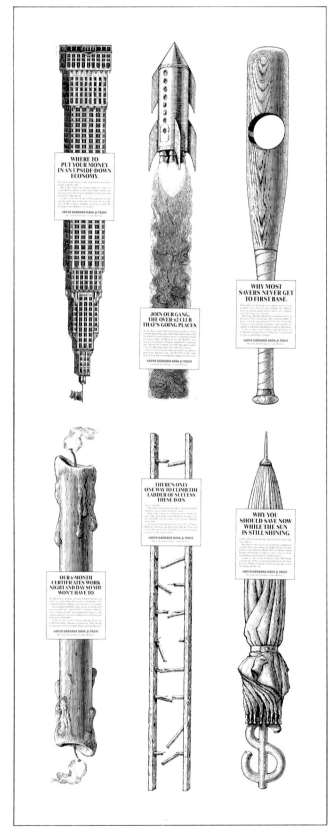

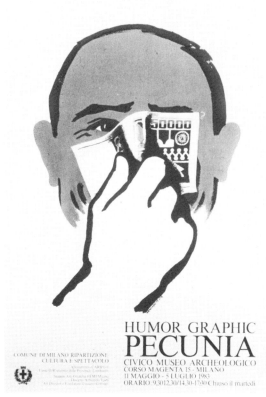

Problem: Create an illustration poking
fun at the state of currency values.
Artist: Armando Testa
Art Director: Armando Testa
Publication: Humor Graphic, Milan

Problem: Illustrate an article on
President Carter's attempts to cut back
on inflation.
Artist: Eugene Mihaesco
Art Director: Eric Seidman
Publication: The New York Times

Problem: Illustrate an article entitled
"Capitalism's Last Gasp."
Artist: Gordon Mortensen
Art Director: Gordon Mortensen
Publication: Skeptic

Problem: Design a symbol to
reflect a bank's increasing
fortunes.
Designer: Bob Dennard
Art Director: Bob Dennard
Client: Mercantile Bank

Problem: Illustrate an article on the
increasing privatization of European
businesses.
Artist: Eugene Mihaesco
Art Director: Rudy Hoglund
Designer: Tom Bentkowski
Publication: Time

Problem: Illustrate an article on
protectionist U.S. territorial fishing laws.
Artist: Henrik Drescher
Art Director: Ronn Campisi
Publication: The Boston Globe Magazine

Education

Enlightenment, Knowledge, Tutorial, Literacy, Erudition, Scholarship, Learning, Culture (See Literature)

The computer has replaced the blackboard in the classroom, but not in the visual lexicon, which also includes the mortarboard and gown as the foremost icons of learning.

Problem: Create a poster announcing a university show of humorous artwork.
Artist: McRay Magleby
Art Director: McRay Magleby
Client: McRay Magleby, Brigham Young University

Problem: Design a poster to promote a college outplacement seminar.
Artist: Gary Viskupic
Art Director: Gary Viskupic
Client: Nassau Community College

Problem: Illustrate a humorous article on yuppie parents and their molding of overachieving children.
Artist: Nurit Karlin
Art Director: Judy Garlan
Publication: The Atlantic

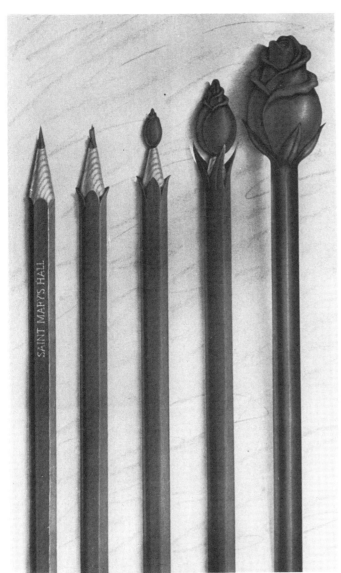

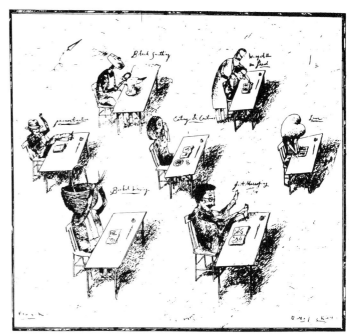

Problem: Illustrate an article on ''silly'' elective courses available to students (at the expense of basic education).
Artist: Henrik Drescher
Art Director: Lynn Staley
Publication: The Boston Globe Magazine

Problem: Design a poster that captures the spirit of and promotes a private girls' school.
Artist: Mark Weakley
Art Director: Barbara Shimkus
Client: Saint Mary's Hall

Problem: Design a cover for a promotional brochure for an art school.
Artist: Robert Shelley
Art Director: Domenica Genovese
Designer: Robert Shelley
Client: The Corcoran School of Art

Energy

Power, Force, Current, Potency, Verve, Vigor, Dash (See Atomic, Technology)

Dinosaur fuels were once the world's primary energy source, so depictions of oil and coal energy sources were rather simple. Electricity was also easy to illustrate as a lightning bolt or turbo. Today the invisible man-made energy sources pose visual challenges.

Problem: Design a symbol for an oil firm.
Art Director: Jerry Choat
Designer: Jerry Choat
Client: Gem State Petroleum

Problem: Design a symbol for an oil and gas firm.
Art Director: Luis D. Acevedo
Designer: Luis D. Acevedo
Client: Stallworth Oil & Gas Inc.

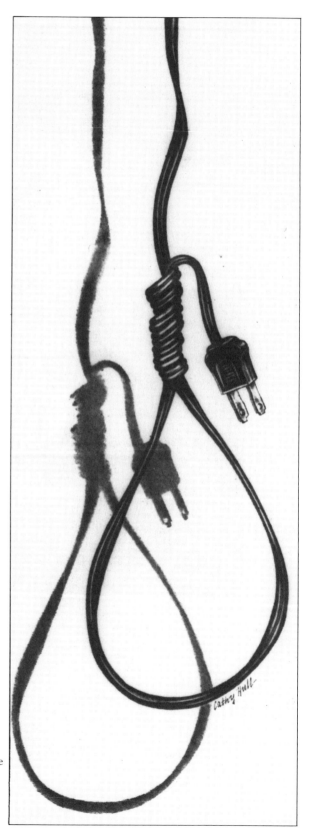

Problem: Illustrate an article on the problem of overdependence on electricity.
Artist: Cathy Hull
Art Director: Bob Eisner
Publication: The New York Times

Problem: Design a symbol for an energy company.
Artist: Unknown
Art Director: The Richards Group
Client: Crown Energy Company

Barbara Lowery

Problem: Design a jacket for a children's book on oil.
Artists: Nancy Tafuri and Thomas Tafuri
Art Director: Judy Mills
Client: Franklin Watts (publisher)

Problem: Design a poster announcing a design exhibition.
Artist: Shigeo Fukuda
Art Director: Shigeo Fukuda
Client: Japan Design Committee

Problem: Illustrate an article on the origins of petroleum.
Artist: Jose Cruz
Art Director: Judy Garlan
Publication: The Atlantic

Environment

Surroundings, Habitat, Atmosphere, Climate, Context, Earth (See Nature)

The Tree of Life was once the primary environmental symbol. With the planet in a constant state of man-made upheaval, environmental critiques are more complex and severe.

Problem: Illustrate an article on the state of farming today.
Artist: Tom Curry
Art Director: Susan McClellan
Designer: Gordon Mortensen
Publication: Harrowsmith

Problem: Create a book jacket depicting environmental concerns and the environmentally negative "engineering" mentality.
Artist: Don Ivan Punchatz
Art Director: Barbara Bertoli
Designer: Don Ivan Punchatz
Client: Avon Books

Problem: Illustrate an article on the dangers of pesticide-laden foods.
Artist: Ignacio Gomez
Art Director: Arthur Paul
Publication: Playboy

52

ENVIRONMENT

Problem: Create cover art for a
publication on the environment.
Photographer: George Arakaki
Art Director: Saul Bass
Client: AT&T

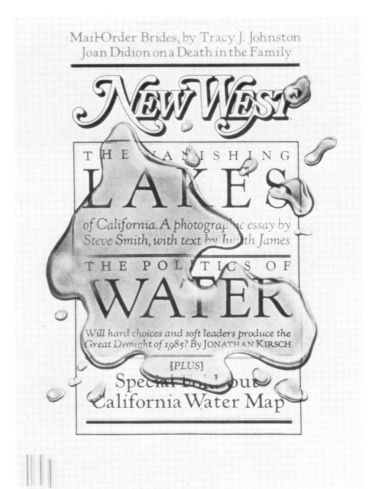

Mail-Order Brides, by Tracy J. Johnston
Joan Didion on a Death in the Family

NEW WEST

THE VANISHING
LAKES
of California. A photographic essay by
Steve Smith, with text by Judith James

THE POLITICS OF
WATER

Will hard choices and soft leaders produce the
Great Drought of 1985? By JONATHAN KIRSCH

{PLUS}

Special Pull-Out
California Water Map

Problem: Design a magazine cover for a
feature issue on water.
Artist: Roger Black
Art Director: Roger Black
Designer: Michael Salisbury
Publication: New West

Problem: Illustrate an article on the
potential danger of uncontrolled use of
genetically engineered microbial
pesticides.
Artist: John Segal
Art Director: Mike Todd
Publication: The New York Times

Problem: Design a logo for the Society of
Environmental Graphic Designers.
Artist: Doug Akagi
Art Director: Doug Akagi
Designer: Jeffrey Corbin
Client: Society of Environmental Graphic
Designers

Environment

Problem: Design a poster commentary on contemporary urban living.
Artist: Bozema Jankowska
Clients: U. W. Olsztyn, Bolestaw Karpowicz, and Krystyna Rutkowska

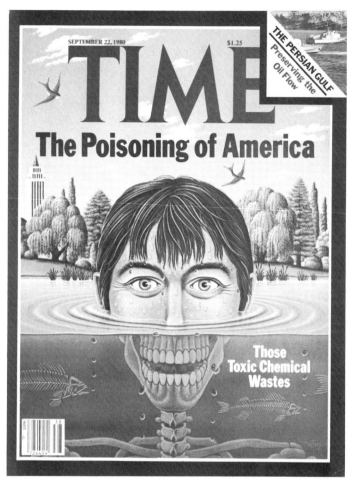

Problem: Create a cover illustration highlighting a feature article on the poisoning of America's waters with toxic wastes.
Artist: James Marsh
Art Director: Nigel Holmes
Publication: Time

Problem: Depict a society in decay, casting off old elements and revelling in strife and competition.
Artist: Hans Georg Rauch
Art Director: Hans Georg Rauch
Client: Prestel-Verlag

Problem: Design a line of generic-product packages easily differentiated from other "generic" packages.
Art Director: Michael Peters
Designer: Bev Whitehead
Client: Yellow Can Company

Famous

Star, Celebrity, Notorious, Popular, Prominent, Distinguished

A portrait need not be the classic face but a caricature that expresses both the inner and outer characteristics of the personality.

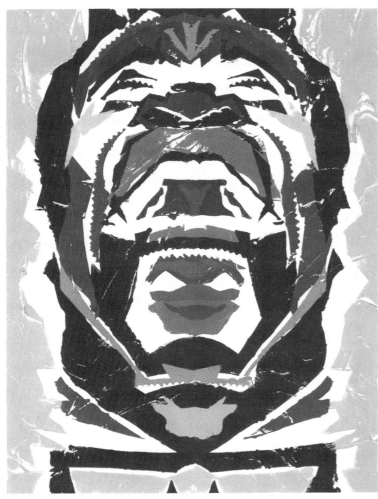

Problem: Create a portrait of B. B. King for a jazz festival promotional poster.
Artist: Ian Wright
Art Director: Rip Georges
Client: Playboy Jazz Festival

Problem: Create a portrait of Tina Turner.
Artist: Blair Drawson
Art Director: Derek Hughes
Publication: Rolling Stone

Problem: Create a portrait of Tom Wolfe to accompany a book review.
Artist: Mark D. Summers
Art Director: Steven Heller
Publication: The New York Times Book Review

夢と魔法の夏休み。 Tokyo Disneyland

Problem: Create a poster image for Tokyo Disneyland.
Artist: Akira Yokoyama
Art Director: Keiji Iijima
Designer: Masahiko Oba
Client: Oriental Land Corp., Ltd.

Famous

Problem: Illustrate the theme "Roy Rogers and Other Heroes of the Sagebrush."
Artist: David Calderley
Art Director: David Calderley
Client: Unpublished.

Problem: Create a poster promoting a Shakespeare festival and depicting Shakespeare as an integral part of daily life.
Artist: John Martin
Art Director: Richard Clewes
Client: The Stratford Festival, Ontario

Problem: Create an advertising poster for a Woody Allen film.
Artist: Gábor Gyárfás
Art Director: Agnes Farago
Client: Mowép

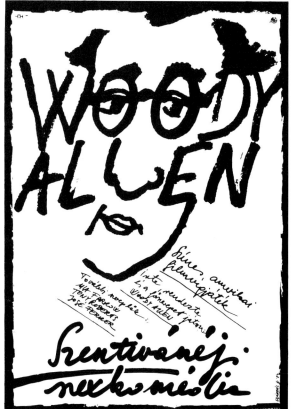

Problem: Illustrate famous future-thinkers in the manner of the predicting devices that made them famous.
Artist: Dave Stevenson
Art Director: Kit Hinrichs
Client: Simpson Paper Company

Problem: Create a portrait of Ray Charles.
Artist: Anita Kunz
Art Director: Fred Woodward
Publication: Texas Monthly

Problem: Create a self-promotional stationery piece.
Art Director/Designer: George Snow
Client: George Snow

Problem: Depict Fidel Castro in a way that will emphasize his role as a Soviet pawn.
Artist: Gordon Mortensen
Art Director: Gordon Mortensen
Publication: Skeptic

Fashion

People wear clothes, but they buy fashion. Fashion is the style of the moment. Its nature is transitory, yet it is recurrent. Its exaggerated symbols are often the most honestly representative.

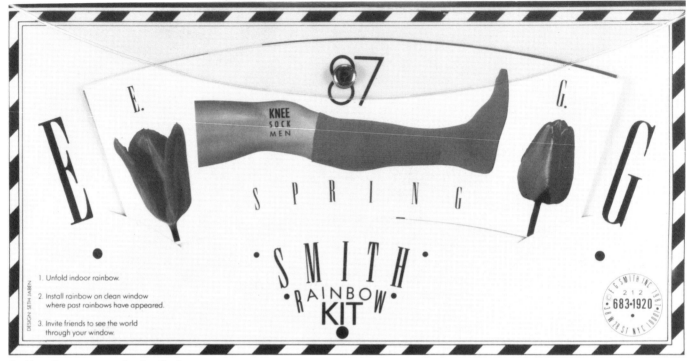

Problem: Create a promotional mailer/in-store display for a sock company.
Artist: Seth Jaben
Art Director: Seth Jaben
Client: E. G. Smith Rainbow Sock Company

Problem: Create a logo for a laundry and dry cleaning company.
Art Director: Don Arday
Designer: Don Arday
Client: Manhattan Laundry & Dry Cleaning

Problem: Create a mark for a liturgical vestment designer.
Artist: Gregory Cutshaw
Art Director: Gregory Cutshaw
Client: Tom Vails, Liturgical Vestment Designer

Great Coats

In Which We Demonstrate How Coated Papers From Champion Capture the Imagination

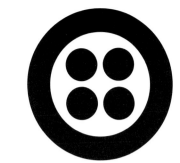

Problem: Create a mark for a men's clothing organization.
Art Director: Stan Richards
Designer: Stan Richards
Client: Sanford Saks

Problem: Create a whimsical illustration to promote coated papers.
Artist: Edward Koren
Art Director: James Miho
Client: Champion Paper

Problem: Create an illustration for an advertisement for men's trousers.
Artist: Elwood H. Smith
Art Director: James Noel Smith
Publication: Dallas Times Herald, Dallas City

Fashion

Problem: Create a mark for use by a sportswear firm.
Artist: Vigon Seireeni
Art Director: Vigon Seireeni
Client: Gotcha Sportswear

Problem: Create a symbol for the "Bourgeois Communist Party."
Artist: Rich Mahon
Art Director: Vigon Seireeni
Client: Vigon Seireeni

Problem: Create a mark for a swimwear line.
Artist: Vigon Seireeni
Art Director: Vigon Seireeni
Client: Barely Legal

Problem: Illustrate a magazine feature article on the popularity of T-shirts.
Artist: Ri Kaiser
Art Director: W. Behnken
Publication: Stern

Film

*Cinema, Movies, Celluloid, Flick,
Motion Picture, Photoplay, Hollywood
(See Art)*

The accoutrements of film are among
the most visually accessible: movie
cameras on tripods, film sprockets,
cans of film, and the director's chair
are the twentieth-century equivalents
of the masks of drama and comedy.

Problem: Design a humorous, attention-
grabbing personnel recruitment ad.
Artist: Gary Templin
Art Director: Gary Templin
Client: The James Gang

Problem: Design a poster and program
cover for the print promotion campaign
for the United States Film Festival.
Art Director: Marcus Nispel
Designer: Marcus Nispel
Client: Sundance Institute

Problem: Design an ad for a series of
films shown on television in tribute to
Alfred Hitchcock on his eightieth
birthday.
Artist: Peter Brookes
Art Director: Brian Thomas
Publication: Radio Times, London

Film

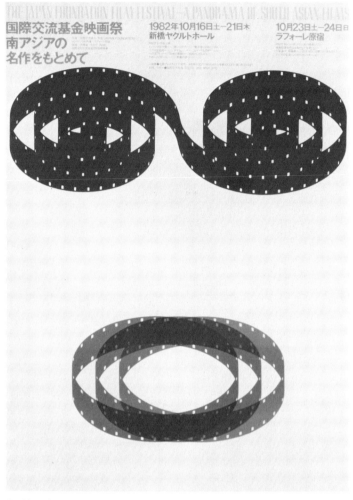

Problem: Create a promotional poster for
the Tenth Annual Los Angeles
International Film Exposition.
Photographer: George Arakaki
Art Director: Saul Bass
Client: Los Angeles International Film
Exposition

Problem: Design a promotional poster for
a festival of South Asian films.
Artist: Shigeo Fukuda
Art Director: Shigeo Fukuda
Client: The Japan Foundation

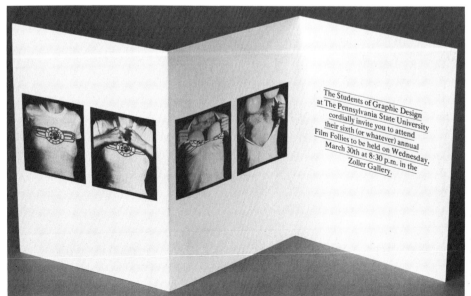

Problem: Design an invitation to a show
of comedic student film work.
Photographer: Bob Borkoski
Art Director: Lanny Sommese
Designers: Jules Epstein and Steve
Zellers
Client: Pennsylvania State University
Graphic Design Department

**Fresh Films
USA Film Festival
March 23 – March 31
Inwood Theater
Dallas, Texas**

Problem: Create a promotional poster for the USA Film Festival.
Artist: Cap Pannell
Art Director: Cap Pannell
Client: USA Film Festival

Problem: Create a poster image to publicize the 1982 Cannes Film Festival.
Artist: Jean-Christian Knaff
Art Director: Yves Desharnais
Client: Publicité Club, Montreal

Problem: Create a logo for the Mill Valley Film Festival.
Artist: John Casado
Art Director: John Casado
Client: Mill Valley Film Festival

Problem: Design a logo for "Festival," a pay-TV network.
Art Director: George Pierson
Designers: George Pierson and Rich Godfrey
Client: Festival Pay-TV

Problem: Design a logo for an international film production company.
Art Director: Michael Peters
Designers: Glenn Tutssel and George Hardie
Client: International Postproduction

Flag

A nation's standard is perhaps the most natural symbol of honor and tool of parody. The Stars and Stripes is a colloquial icon that only the unresourceful imagist fails to use effectively.

Problem: Create a promotional poster for a music festival featuring five American composers.
Artist: Bill Prochnow
Art Director: Bill Prochnow
Client: Cabrillo Music Festival

Problem: Create an illustration, with paper as medium, to be used as part of a promotional calendar for a paper company.
Artist: Carl Seltzer
Art Director: James Cross
Designer: Carl Seltzer
Client: Ingram Paper

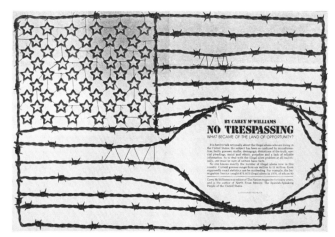

Problem: Illustrate an article on the flow of illegal aliens over U.S. borders.
Artist: Fred Nelson
Art Director: Gordon Mortensen
Publication: Skeptic

Problem: Design an album cover for an anthology of Glenn Miller recordings popular during World War II.
Artist: Art Chantry
Art Director: Art Chantry
Client: First American Records, Inc.

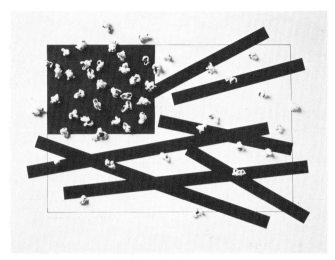

Problem: Interpret the American flag for
an AIGA show and subsequent book.
Artist: Carl Seltzer
Art Director: Carl Seltzer
Client: AIGA/San Francisco

Problem: Interpret the American flag for
an AIGA show and subsequent book.
Artist: Dugald Stermer
Art Director: Dugald Stermer
Client: AIGA/San Francisco

Problem: Interpret the American flag for
an AIGA show and subsequent book.
Artist: Richard Danne
Art Director: Richard Danne
Client: American Institute of Graphic
Arts/San Francisco

Problem: Interpret the American flag for
an AIGA show and subsequent book.
Artist: John McConnell
Art Director: John McConnell
Client: AIGA/San Francisco

Problem: Interpret the American flag for
an AIGA show and subsequent book.
Artist: McRay Magleby
Art Director: McRay Magleby
Client: AIGA/San Francisco

Problem: Interpret the American flag for
an AIGA show and subsequent book.
Artist: Craig Frazier
Art Director: Craig Frazier
Client: AIGA/San Francisco

Food

The preparation and eating of food are events of ritualistic proportions. Attention to diet and fascination with haute cuisine have made the subject of food a requisite of publishing.

Problem: Design a brunch menu for a restaurant catering to a youthful clientele.
Art Director: Luis D. Acevedo
Designer: Luis D. Acevedo
Client: T.G.I. Friday's

Problem: Design an invitation to a sushi dinner party.
Art Director: Bruce Rubin
Designer: Jim Cordaro
Clients: Susan, Bruce, Bruce, and Jim

The glorious presentation of Japanese cuisine. Experience the taste, texture, aroma and aesthetic presentation of the impeccably freshest and best of the market place. You are cordially invited by Susan, Bruce, Bruce and Jim to an evening of adventure on Saturday, December 1, 1984 7pm 115 N 1st St. in Minneapolis. 3rd floor loft. Guests may bring beers and dry white wines to heighten the delightful sensations.

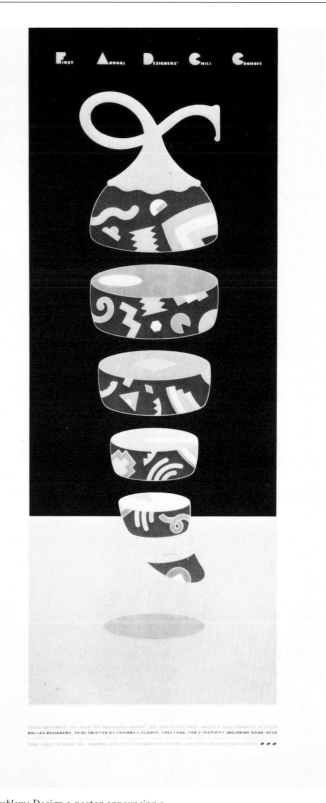

Problem: Design a poster announcing a chili cook-off between Dallas-area design firms.
Artist: Rex Peteet
Art Director: Bob Dennard
Client: Dallas area design community

Problem: Transform the ordinary American breakfast into the high-tech breakfast of the future.
Artist: Dave Jonason
Art Director: Dave Jonason
Client: Self-promotion

Problem: Design a mark for the Lone Star Donuts Chain.
Artist: John Evans
Art Director: Rex Peteet
Designer: Rex Peteet
Client: Lone Star Donuts

THE   STUFF   OF   LIFE

IN PURSUIT OF THE WELL-BALANCED DIET

Original.   Chunky.

Whether you choose our original sauce with imported olive oil and romano cheese, or our chunky homestyle with bits of tomato, herbs and spices, you'll get classic Italian taste.

PRINCE

Problem: Create art for an advertisement praising the virtues of thicker spaghetti sauce.
Artist: Mark Hess
Art Director: Bob Barrie
Client: Prince Spaghetti

Problem: Design an attractive, nutritionally educational calendar.
Art Directors: Gary Fritts and William Hanna
Designers: Gary Fritts, William Hanna, Carolyn Bauman, and Julie Sanner
Client: St. Vincent's Health Center

Food

Problem: Create an illustration for a guide to uncommon European cooking.
Artist: Jose Cruz
Art Director: Rhoda Gubernick
Publication: The Atlantic

Problem: Illustrate an article on appetite regulation.
Artist: Lonnie Sue Johnson
Art Director: Tina Adamek
Publication: Postgraduate Medicine

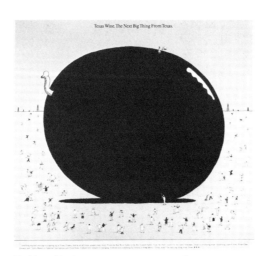

Problem: Design a poster to promote the fledgling Texas wine industry.
Artist: Ken Koester
Art Director: Ken Koester
Client: Texas Department of Agriculture

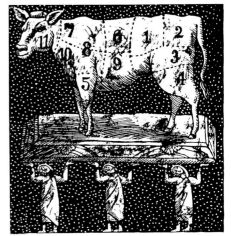

Problem: Illustrate an article on the history of nomad cooking.
Artist: Normand Cousineau
Art Director: Gianni Caccia
Publication: Vice Versa

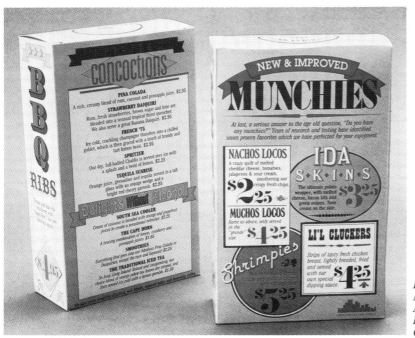

Problem: Create a symbol for worldwide use to communicate the identity of an international commodities organization.
Art Director: Michael Peters
Designer: Madeleine Bennett
Client: International Coffee Organization

Problem: Design an attractive, uniquely American menu which involves the diner.
Art Director: Paisley-Ramorini
Designer: Paisley-Ramorini
Client: Mardeck, Ltd.

Problem: Design a "to go" menu for a popular restaurant chain.
Artist: Woody Pirtle
Art Director: Woody Pirtle
Client: T.G.I. Friday's/Dalts

Problem: Illustrate an article on nouvelle cuisine as "wimp food."
Artist: Sandra Hendler
Art Director: Tom Staebler
Publication: Playboy

Food

Problem: Create an illustration for a brunch guide.
Artist: Peter Sis
Art Director: Kevin Cody
Publication: Easy Rider

Problem: Create an illustration to accompany an article on myths, misconceptions, and old wives' tales about wine.
Artist: Mark Kseniak
Art Director: Marlowe Goodson
Publication: Attenzione

Problem: Create art to accompany a restaurant review.
Artist: Ken Rinciari
Art Director: Matthew Drace
Publication: San Francisco Focus

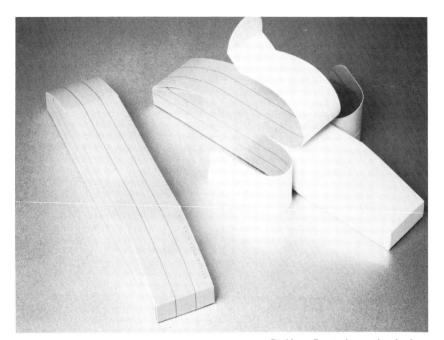

Problem: Create innovative food packaging that resembles the food enclosed.
Artist: Katsu Kimura
Art Director: Katsu Kimura
Client: Personal design experiment

Problem: Illustrate an article giving "sophisticated" recipes using peanut butter.
Artist: Renée Klein
Art Director: Ronn Campisi
Publication: The Boston Globe

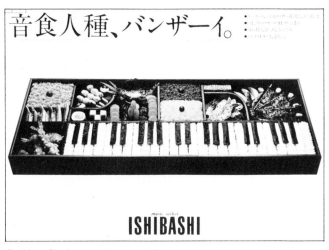

音食人種、バンザーイ。

music seeker
ISHIBASHI

Problem: Design a poster promoting
Japanese-made electronic keyboards.
Artist: Sachiko Ito
Photographer: Kazuhiko Yoshino
Art Director: Masayoshi Koide
Designers: Masayoshi Koide and
Aruji Harada
Client: Ishibashi Musical Instruments
Manufacturing Co.

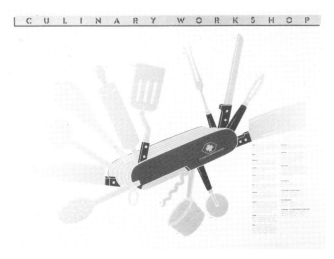

Problem: Create a promotional piece for
a photographer.
Art Director: Frank Tedesco
Designer: Mel Hioko
Client: Frank Tedesco Photography

Problem: Design a poster promoting a
culinary workshop.
Artist: Larry McEntire
Art Director: Tom Poth
Designer: Mike Hicks
Client: St. David's Hospital Culinary
Workshop

Problem: Create a name and trademark
for a chain of Los Angeles–style fast-food
restaurants.
Artist: Marty Neumeier
Art Director: Marty Neumeier
Client: Eatz Restaurants

Problem: Design a poster promotion for
a food service's summer menus featuring
fruits and vegetables.
Artist: Jon Rawson
Art Director: Amy Reynolds
Client: Szabo Food Service

Health

Medicine conjures up images of hospital beds, X-rays, and doctors' bags. In the current age of specialization, these images are not sufficient to represent the full range of health care.

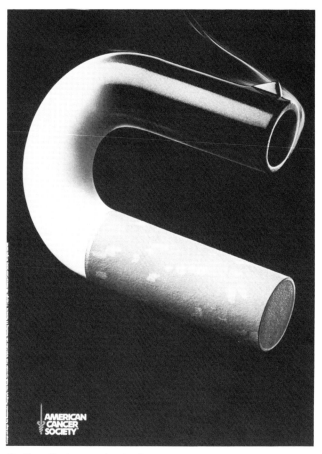

Problem: Design a poster for the American Cancer Society to promote an antismoking campaign.
Photographer: Nick Koudis
Art Director: Bob Boezewinkel
Client: American Cancer Society

Problem: Design a poster to promote the American Cancer Society's national "smoke out."
Artist: Seymour Chwast
Art Director: Seymour Chwast
Client: American Cancer Society

Problem: Illustrate an editorial on the dangers to nonsmokers of breathing "secondary smoke."
Artist: Douglas Florian
Art Director: Jerelle Kraus
Publication: The New York Times

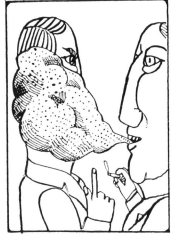

Problem: Create an editorial illustration for an article on skin bacteria.
Artist: Seth Jaben
Art Director: Tina Adamek
Publication: Postgraduate Medicine

Problem: Create a logo for a chain of
weight-reduction centers.
Designer: Steven P. Miller
Art Director: Stan Richards
Client: Slimway

Problem: Create a jacket for a book on
fitness and American society.
Artist: John Craig
Art Director: Louise Fili
Client: Pantheon Books

Problem: Illustrate an editorial on the
dangers of smoking.
Artist: Horacio Fidel Cardo
Art Director: Horacio Fidel Cardo
Client: Ciencia Supplement, Clarin

Problem: Illustrate an article on the
stigma facing workers with AIDS.
Artist: Dave Shannon
Art Director: John White
Publication: Time

Problem: Illustrate an article on the
effects of traumatic head injuries.
Artist: Edward Koren
Art Director: Josh Gosfield
Publication: New York

Health

Problem: Illustrate an article on the effects of toxic mercury levels in the workplace.
Artist: Normand Cousineau
Art Director: Patrick J. B. Flynn
Publication: The Progressive

Problem: Design a promotional piece for the student health service at the University of Utah.
Artists: Bill Swenson, Micheal Richards, Scott Greer
Art Director: Micheal Richards
Designers: Micheal Richards and Bill Swenson
Client: University of Utah Division of Continuing Education

Problem: Create accompanying art for an article on headaches.
Artist: Michael Bartolos
Art Director: Robert Best
Publication: New York

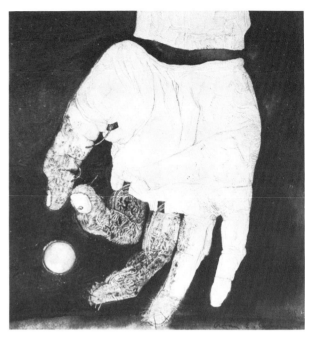

Problem: Create an editorial illustration for an article on Carpal Tunnel Syndrome, a nerve dysfunction affecting the hand.
Artist: Alan Cober
Art Director: Tina Adamek
Publication: Postgraduate Medicine

Problem: Illustrate an article on infertility problems related to the workplace.
Artist: Bascove
Art Director: Patrick J. B. Flynn
Publication: The Progressive

Human Relations

Interaction, Emotions, Passions, Conflicts, Relationships

Love, hate, happiness, and sadness are aspects of human relations most commonly visualized. Direct depictions of emblematic facial characteristics and symbolic references using classical metaphors are most prevalent.

Problem: Illustrate an article on the fear of flying.
Artist: Robert Neubecker
Art Directors: Theodore Kalamarakis and Eric Seidman
Publication: Discover

Problem: Illustrate an article on controlling anger.
Artist: Earl Keleny
Art Director: Alice Degenhardt
Publication: Creative Living

Problem: Illustrate an editorial on the tightly leashed violence of revolutionary political movements.
Artist: Horacio Fidel Cardo
Art Director: Jerelle Kraus
Publication: The New York Times

Human Relations

Problem: Illustrate a greeting card depicting love as a universal emotion.
Artist: Sadahito Mori
Art Director: Sadahito Mori
Client: Verkere Reprodukties BV, Holland

Problem: Illustrate an article on how men deal with failed love relationships.
Artist: Mark Penberthy
Art Director: Ken Kendrick
Publication: The New York Times Magazine

Problem: Illustrate a poem by Jacques Prévert.
Artist: Henri Galeron
Art Director: Pierre Marchand
Client: Editions Gallimard

RAPPORT

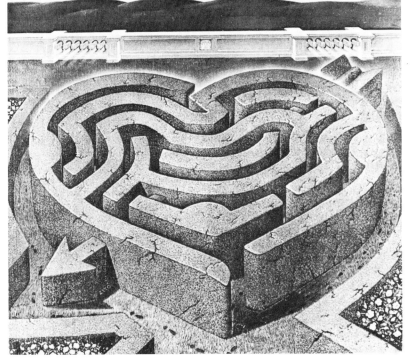

Problem: Illustrate an article on the heartbreak of lost love and the incapacitating effect of lovesickness.
Artist: Dagmar Frinta
Art Director: Carl Stein
Publication: Intro

Problem: Design a jacket for an album entitled "Learning to Love."
Artist: Andy Zito
Art Director: Nancy Donald
Client: CBS Records

Problem: Design a masthead/logo for a financial adviser's company publication.
Artist: Dave Epstein
Art Director: Dave Epstein
Client: Dawson-O'Day & Co.

Problem: Depict the depth of responsibility in true friendship (book jacket for Franz Kafka's *The Trial*).
Artist: Jarmila Maranova
Art Director: Michael Mendelsohn
Client: The Franklin Library

Human Relations

Problem: Illustrate an article on stress.
Artist: Eugene Mihaesco
Art Director: Tina Adamek
Designer: Nancy Rice
Publication: Postgraduate Medicine

Problem: Depict the heartbreak of failed relationships.
Artist: Henrik Drescher
Art Director: Unknown
Client: Unknown

Problem: Illustrate late-night loneliness.
Artist: Brenda Lee Tracy
Art Director: Brenda Lee Tracy
Client: Unpublished

Illusion

Deception, Appearance, Superficiality, Mirage, Phantasm, Hallucination, Misimpression

Now you see it; now you don't. Illusion is magic, promise, and deceit. Illusion is also the linchpin of most conceptual ideas, with surrealism a common means of creating the effect.

Problem: Illustrate an article on the dangers of high speed limits.
Artist: Guy Billout
Art Director: Judy Garlan
Publication: The Atlantic

Problem: Create a stationery system and promotion piece for a graphic design studio.
Art Director/Designer: Sachi Kuwihara
Client: Sawchees Studio (owner is Sachi Kuwihara; Sachi is pronounced *Saw-Chee*)

Problem: Illustrate an article on secrecy versus democracy and effective political use of information.
Artist: Bob Gale
Art Director: Renée Klein
Publication: Time

Illusion

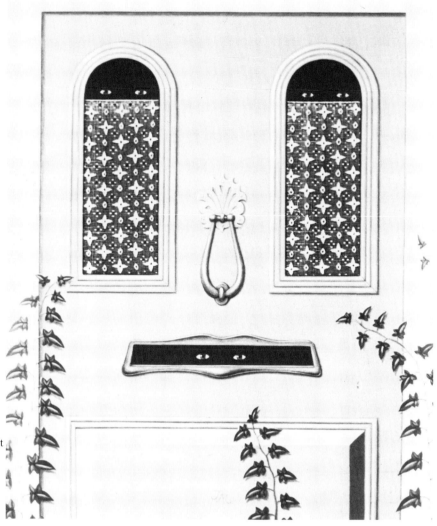

Problem: Create a book jacket image that is more than it appears to be, and that produces a sense of curiosity and foreboding in the reader.
Artist: James Marsh
Art Director: David Pelham
Client: Penguin Books

Problem: Illustrate an editorial piece on the medical profession's love of "zebras," or unlikely and unusual diagnoses.
Artist: Marian Christopher Zacharow
Art Director: Eric Seidman
Publication: Discover

Industry

Work, Toil, Enterprise, Commerce, Trade (See Business, Economy, and Technology)

During the mid-nineteenth century the smokestack was the perjorative symbol of industrialization. Later it became the emblem of progress, along with the crucible, assembly line, and computer.

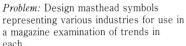

Problem: Design masthead symbols representing various industries for use in a magazine examination of trends in each.
Artist: Douglas Fraser
Art Directors: Malcolm Frouman and Mitch Shostak
Designer: Sharon Bystrek
Publication: Business Week

Problem: Illustrate an article on America's increasing industrial development.
Artist: Mark Hess
Art Director: Margery Peters
Publication: Fortune (illustration not used)

Industry

Problem: Illustrate a profile of five of America's best-run family businesses.
Artist: Mirko Ilic
Art Director: Steven Heller
Publication: The New York Times Book Review

Problem: Design a logo for a pretzel machine company.
Artist: Jack Gernsheimer
Art Director: Jack Gernsheimer
Client: Reading Pretzel Machinery Company, Inc., Reading, PA

Problem: Design a logo for a maker of plastic fibers used in carpets and draperies.
Art Director: Don Weller
Designers: Don Weller, Dennis Juett, and Chikako Matsubayashi
Client: Polyfibres, Inc.

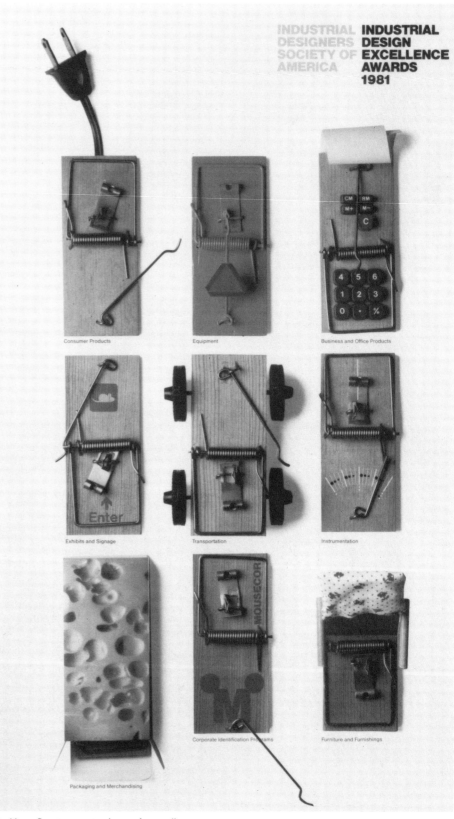

INDUSTRIAL DESIGNERS SOCIETY OF AMERICA

INDUSTRIAL DESIGN EXCELLENCE AWARDS 1981

Consumer Products

Equipment

Business and Office Products

Exhibits and Signage

Transportation

Instrumentation

Packaging and Merchandising

Corporate Identification Programs

Furniture and Furnishings

Problem: Create a poster image for a call for entries for the Industrial Designers Society of America competition.
Artist: Bart Crosby
Art Director: Bart Crosby
Client: Industrial Designers Society of America

Problem: Design a logo for a construction company.
Artist: Woody Pirtle
Art Director: Woody Pirtle
Client: Travis Construction Company

Problem: Design a trademark for an electrical contractor.
Artist: Don Weller
Art Director: Don Weller
Client: Bergelectric Corp.

Problem: Design a logo for an architectural/contracting firm.
Artist: Dave Epstein
Art Director: Dave Epstein
Client: Design & Construct Associates

Problem: Create a logo for a custom cabinetmaker.
Artist: Dave Epstein
Art Director: Dave Epstein
Client: United Woodworks, Inc.

Problem: Illustrate an article on the rebirth of the U.S. Steel Company.
Artist: Robert Crawford
Art Director: John McLaughlin
Publication: Financial World

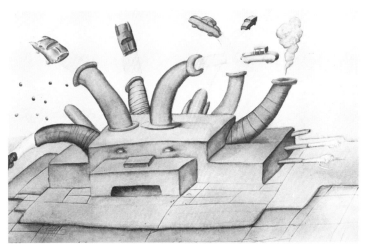

Problem: Illustrate the rote nature of American auto production.
Artist: Jeff Kronen
Art Director: Jeff Kronen
Client: Self-promotion

Problem: Create magazine cover art for a feature story on the automated factories of the future.
Artist: Michael Schwab
Art Director: Hall Kelley
Designer: Michael Schwab
Publication: Solutions

Intelligence

Smarts, Knowledge, Moxie, Brains, Wits, Wisdom, Know-how, Ability, Sagacity, Acumen, I.Q. (See Education, Memory, Science, Technology)

The brain is the basic symbol for intelligence. In medieval times, eyeglasses were used to depict scholars and wise men. In the cartoonist's and advertiser's lexicon, the light bulb describes the smart idea.

Problem: Create a book jacket for a "culture test."
Artist: Steven Guarnaccia
Art Director: Joseph Montebello
Designer: Steven Guarnaccia
Client: Harper & Row

Problem: Create an editorial illustration for an anthology on "owls" (symbols of wisdom).
Artist: Peter Brookes
Art Director: Nick Thirkell
Client: W. H. Allen Publishers

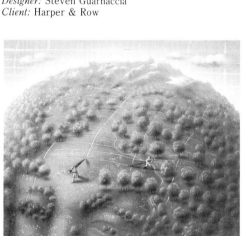

Problem: Illustrate an article on thinking in two dimensions.
Artist: Kinuko Craft
Art Director: Deborah Flynn-Hanrahan
Publication: Lotus

Problem: Create cover art for a magazine special issue on what "smart" New Yorkers do.
Artist: Michael Economy
Art Director: Richard Pandiscio
Designer: Kim Hastreiter
Client: Paper Publishing

Literature

Writing, Prose, Letters, Classics, Novels (See Art, Education)

Books and their makers are often the subjects of editorial enquiry and critique. The classic images of the bard and laurel leaf are in currency today. Yet even as shorthand they are much too simplistic.

Problem: Illustrate a review of a work chronicling James Joyce's Dublin.
Artist: Martim Avillez
Art Director: Deborah Rust
Publication: Harper's

Problem: Design a symbol for the New Canaan Library, incorporating both books and leaves, which reflects the Connecticut countryside.
Artist: Don Ervin
Art Director: Don Ervin
Client: New Canaan Library

Problem: Graphically depict the power of international communication.
Artist: Jeff Denning
Art Director: Jeff Denning
Client: Baxter + Korge (company Christmas card)

Literature

Problem: Illustrate an article entitled
"Never Cry Author" about the
difficulties in translating written work
intact to the screen.
Artist: Henrik Drescher
Art Director: Elizabeth Vanitalie
Publication: The Movies

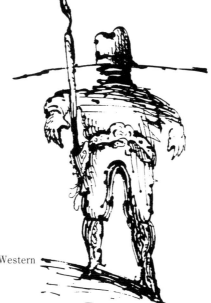

Problem: Illustrate an article on Western
authors.
Artist: Ken Rinciari
Art Director: John Beveridge
Publication: American Film

Problem: Design a logo/trademark for an
international women's writing guild.
Artist: D. Bruce Zahor
Art Director: D. Bruce Zahor
Client: International Women's Writing Guild

Problem: Create a symbol/mark for a "nonsense book."
Artist: U. G. Sato
Art Director: U. G. Sato
Client: Shisaku Publishing Company, Ltd.

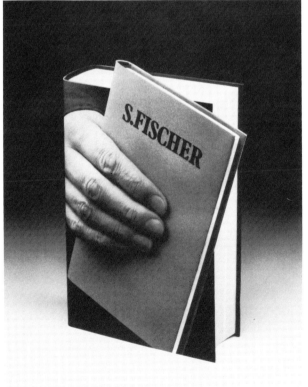

GARY

Problem: Create a logo for Gary Gray, a copywriter.
Artist: Woody Pirtle
Art Director: Woody Pirtle
Client: Gary Gray

Problem: Design a series of book covers
Artist: Gunther Rambow
Art Director: Gunther Rambow
Client: S. Fischer

Marriage and Divorce

Trouble and Strife, Ball and Chain, Wedlock, Matrimony, Conjugality, Union, Espousal, Dissolution, Split, Disunion, Separation, Divide, Annul (See Human Relations, Sex)

A sacred heart represents marriage in Ireland, while a split, tattered one indicates its converse in other Western countries. The ring, wedding cake, and Cupid are among the most common symbols used and abused.

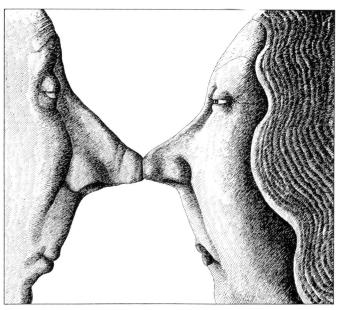

Problem: Create an illustration for a poster promoting a play entitled *Bedroom Farce*.
Artist: Fred Hilliard
Art Director: Fred Hilliard
Client: Seattle Repertory Theatre

Problem: Illustrate an editorial on modern American wedding rites.
Artist: Buddy Hickerson
Art Director: James Noel Smith
Publication: Westward Magazine, Dallas Times Herald

Problem: Illustrate an article entitled "Ground Rules for a Fair Divorce."
Artist: Brian Ajhar
Art Director: Unknown
Publication: Business Week

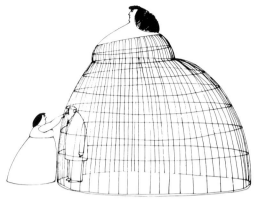

Problem: Draw a humorous depiction of relationships between men and women.
Artist: Paul Flora
Art Director: Unknown
Client: Unknown

Problem: Illustrate an article on communication between the sexes.
Artist: Anita Kunz
Art Director: Jackie Young
Publication: Financial Post

Problem: Illustrate an article on fathers being awarded custody of their children.
Artist: Buddy Hickerson
Art Director: Buddy Hickerson
Publication: The Denver Post

Media (Press)

Journalism, Reportage, Television, Coverage, Broadcasting, Print, News, World Opinion (See Art, Film, Music, Theatre)

With the advent of electronic media, the lexicon of media symbols has grown to include many of the devices used to transmit information. Antennae, microphones, and cathode ray tubes are but a few of the tools.

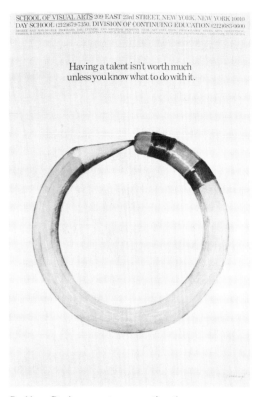

Problem: Design a poster promoting the School of Visual Arts.
Artist: Tony Palladino
Art Director: Silas Rhodes
Designer: Tony Palladino
Client: School of Visual Arts Press

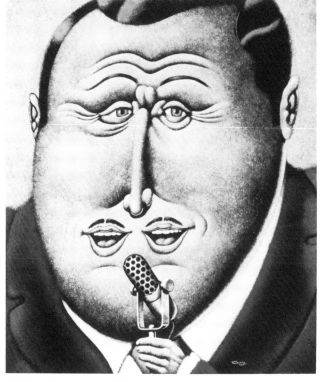

Problem: Illustrate an article on television newscasters who repeat themselves to fill air time.
Artist: Tom Curry
Art Director: Greg Paul
Publication: Plain Dealer

Problem: Design a business card for a voice talent who performs other services.
Artist: Tom Varisco
Art Director: Tom Varisco
Client: Ken Hanson

Problem: Illustrate an article on the adverse effects of television on children.
Artist: Stuart Goldenberg
Art Director: Pam Vassil
Publication: The New York Times

Problem: Create jacket art for a book
entitled *The Engineer of Human Souls*.
Artist: Fred Marcellino
Art Director: Sara Eisenman
Designer: Fred Marcellino
Client: Knopf

Problem: Illustrate an article on the
elimination of televisions.
Artist: Sean Early
Art Director: Joe Brooks
Publication: Penthouse

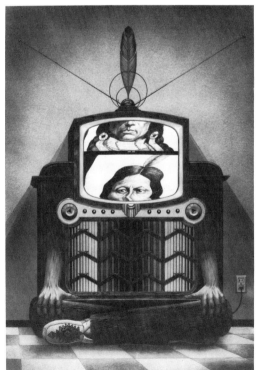

Problem: Design a poster encouraging
political participation.
Artist: Melanie Roher
Art Director: Melanie Roher
Client: Mobil Oil Corporation

Problem: Design a magazine ad
announcing corporate sponsorship of the
MacNeil/Lehrer Report on PBS.
Art Director: Rob Hugel
Designers: Rob Hugel and Patti Levenburg
Client: Herman Miller, Inc.

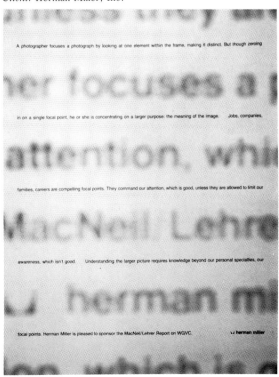

Medicine

Cure, Treatment, Pathology, General Practice (See Health, Mental Health)

Despite advancements in technology, the classic images of the healing profession are still the most common, often shared with health. Yet medicine tends to suggest science and ethics, while health represents a more personal state of affairs.

Problem: Illustrate an article on nature and ethics.
Artist: David Shannon
Art Director: Barbara Nieminen
Designer: David Shannon
Publication: Squibbline (Squibb Corp. publication)

The Burn Center in The Hospital for Plastic and Reconstructive Surgery

Problem: Create a mark for The Burn Center in the Hospital for Plastic and Reconstructive Surgery.
Art Directors: Robert P. Gersin and Ronald H. Wong
Designer: Ronald H. Wong
Client: New York Hospital

Problem: Design a logo for a hospital's pediatric trauma center.
Artist: Danny Kamerath
Art Director: Danny Kamerath
Client: Parkland Pediatric Trauma Center, Parkland Hospital

Problem: Create a logo for an allergy clinic.
Artist: Dan Ruesch
Art Director: Steve Grigg
Designer: Dan Ruesch
Client: Provo Allergy Clinic

Problem: Design a mark for a recruitment agency for hospital administrators.
Artist: Bonnie Segal
Art Director: Bonnie Segal
Client: Medexec

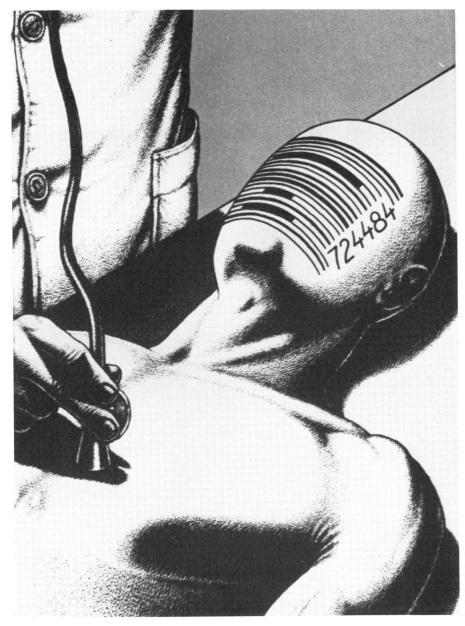

Problem: Illustrate an article reminding physicians that a patient is more than the sum of physical findings.
Artist: Mirko Ilic
Art Director: Eric Seidman
Publication: Discover

Problem: Illustrate an article on for-profit hospitals.
Artist: Henrik Drescher
Art Director: Patrick J. B. Flynn
Publication: The Progressive

Medicine

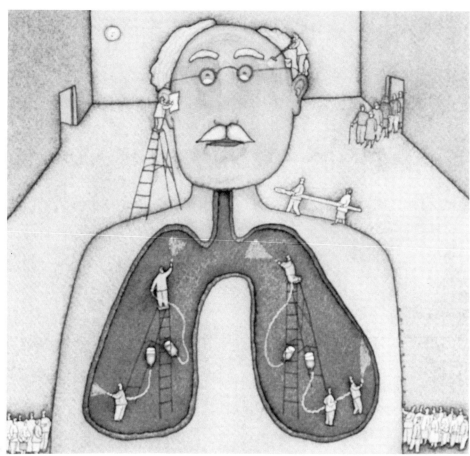

Problem: Illustrate an article on
pneumonia and elderly patients.
Artist: Lonnie Sue Johnson
Art Director: Tina Adamek
Publication: Postgraduate Medicine

Problem: Illustrate an article on
Alzheimer's disease.
Artist: Sandra Filipucci
Art Director: Tina Adamek
Publication: Postgraduate Medicine

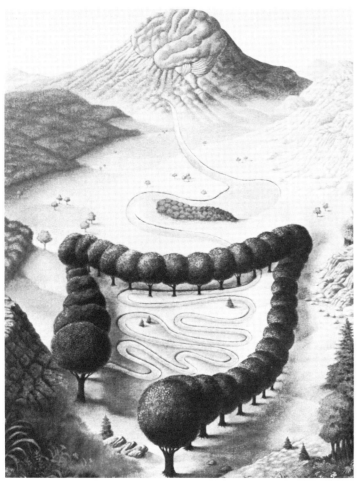

Problem: Create art for an ad for
pharmaceutical products used in treating
digestive disorders.
Artist: Don Ivan Punchatz
Art Director: Al Gardner
Client: Warren Teasdale

Problem: Illustrate an article on
mammalian bites.
Artist: Dale Gottleib
Art Director: Tina Adamek
Publication: Postgraduate Medicine

Problem: Design a mark for a
chiropractic care facility.
Artist: Gregory Cutshaw
Art Director: Gregory Cutshaw
Client: Beno Chiropractic Care

Problem: Create a logo for a general
dentistry practice.
Artist: Mark Freytag
Art Director: Mark Freytag
Client: Freeman and Hendricks, D.D.S.

Problem: Design a trademark for a
medical chemistry firm.
Artist: Félix Beltrán
Art Director: Félix Beltrán
Client: Mediquímica, Havana

Memory

Remembrance, Recall, Retrospection, Souvenir, Keepsake, Retain, Reminiscence (See Aging, Intelligence, Mental Health)

Nostalgia, the romanticization of the past, is that aspect of memory that is most often illustrated. But memory also suggests an act of retrospection, which offers many visual possibilities.

Problem: Design single-image posters to illustrate the themes ''Perspective,'' ''Outline,'' and ''Forget.''
Artist: Kiyuro Yahagi
Art Director: Kiyuro Yahagi
Client: Kiyuro Yahagi (personal project)

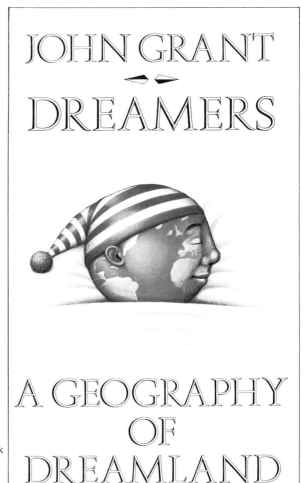

Problem: Create cover art for a book about dreams and the people who dreamed them.
Artist: James Marsh
Art Director: Stephen Abis
Client: Grafton Books

Mental Health

Sanity, Well-being, Balance, Perspective, Playing with a Full Deck, Well-adjusted (See Health, Intelligence, Memory)

Matters of the mind and psyche are often simplistically referred to by the totemic representation of Sigmund Freud. But mental health is more than psychoanalysis alone in joining issues of the mind and heart.

Problem: Illustrate an article describing women who focus on the parts of their bodies with which they are dissatisfied and lose the ability to view themselves as a whole.
Artist: Lynda Gray
Art Director: Pedro Silmon
Publication: The Sunday Times Magazine, The London Times

Problem: Create a poster illustration for *Physicians' Weekly* about "A" type personalities.
Artist: Tom Curry
Art Director: Joe Acree
Publication: Physicians' Weekly

Problem: Design a series of pamphlets advertising the services of a senior citizen network and a suicide prevention center.
Art Director: Michael Sprong
Designer: Michael Sprong
Clients: The East Dallas Senior Citizen Network Youthworks, Inc. and The Suicide and Crisis Center

Mental Health

Problem: Illustrate an article on chemical factors in suicides.
Artist: Dagmar Frinta
Art Director: Mary Challinor
Publication: Science '84

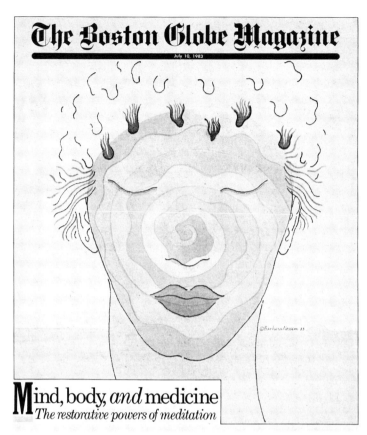

The Boston Globe Magazine
July 10, 1983

Mind, body, *and* medicine
The restorative powers of meditation

Problem: Create magazine cover art for a feature story on the role of meditation in healing.
Artist: Barbara Nessim
Art Director: Ronn Campisi
Publication: The Boston Globe Magazine

Problem: Illustrate an article on self-esteem.
Artist: Barbara Nessim
Art Director: Linda Cox
Publication: Cosmopolitan

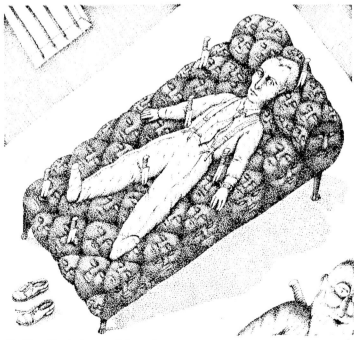

Problem: Illustrate an article on dreams.
Artist: Peter Sis
Art Director: Don Nelson
Publication: Notre Dame

Music

Song, Symphony, Tune, Harmony, Polyphony, Air, Strain, Composition, Notes, Minstrelsy, Ballad, Jazz, Opera, Rock-n-Roll, Serenade (See Art, Media, Theatre)

Few subjects are illustrated in more diversity than music. Few aural arts offer as many graphic images: from musical notes to the instruments to the distinguished visages of the musical masters.

Problem: Design a jacket for an album entitled ''Arthur Blythe: Lenox Avenue Breakdown.''
Artist: Mark Hess
Art Director: Gene Grief
Client: CBS Records

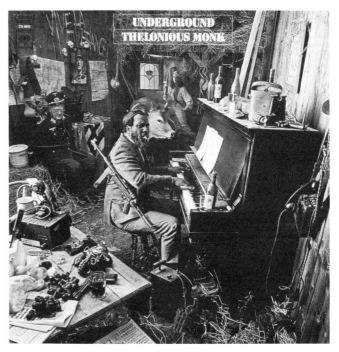

Problem: Design a jacket for an album of ''underground'' jazz recordings by Thelonious Monk.
Art Director: John Berg
Designer: John Berg
Client: Columbia Records

Problem: Design a jacket for a record album entitled ''Concerto Retitled.''
Photographer: Chris Callis
Art Director: Lynn Dreese Breslin
Client: Atlantic Records

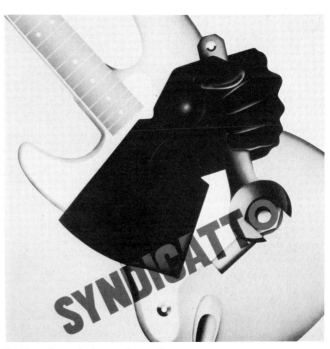

Problem: Create jacket art for an album by a Brazilian rock band.
Artist: Roberto Renner
Art Director: Felipe Taborda
Client: Opus/Columbia Records

Music

Problem: Create a logo for an opera company.
Artist: Woody Pirtle
Art Director: Woody Pirtle
Client: Dallas Opera

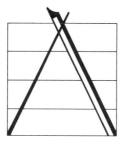

Problem: Create a logo for a symphony orchestra.
Artist: Willie Baronet
Art Director: Willie Baronet
Client: Acadiana Symphony Orchestra

Problem: Design a logo for an airline in-flight music channel.
Art Directors: Arthur Eisenberg and Philip Waugh
Designer: Philip Waugh
Client: Co-op project: Avis/Southwest Airlines

Problem: Design a logo for a New Orleans band.
Artist: Hal Pluché
Art Director: Hal Pluché
Client: Baby Grande

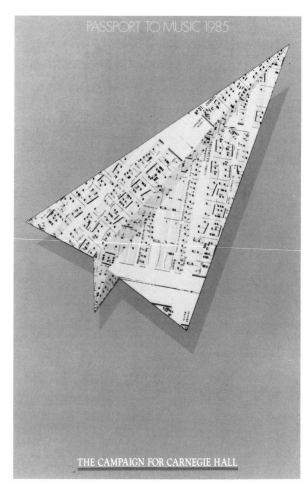

Problem: Design a fund-raising poster for Carnegie Hall.
Artist: Per Arnoldi
Art Director: Per Arnoldi
Client: Carnegie Hall

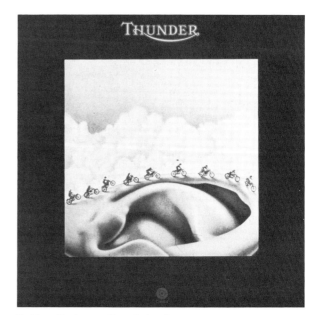

Problem: Design an album jacket for a record entitled "Thunder."
Artist: Bill Jenkins
Art Director: Woody Pirtle
Client: Capitol Records

Problem: Design a jazz promotional
poster.
Artist: Anonymous
Art Director: John Muller
Client: Kansas City Jazz Commission

Problem: Design an invitation to a Dallas
Symphony Orchestra celebration.
Artist: Brian Boyd
Art Director: Brian Boyd
Client: Dallas Symphony Orchestra

Problem: Create jacket art for an album
of Christmas music put out by a radio station.
Artist: Brian Boyd
Art Director: Brian Boyd
Client: KVIL Radio

Problem: Design a jacket for an album
entitled ''Intimate Connection.''
Photographer: Brian Hagiwara
Art Director: Lynn Dreese Breslin
Client: Atlantic Records

Music

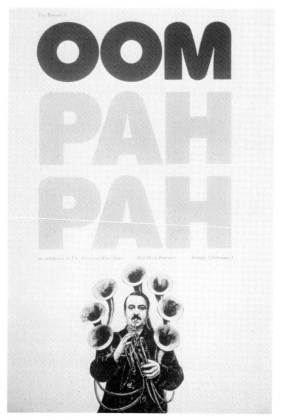

Problem: Design a poster promoting a corporate-sponsored traveling exhibition.
Artist: Melanie Roher
Art Director: Melanie Roher
Client: The Metropolitan Museum of Art

Problem: Illustrate a magazine article on Oscar Peterson, Canadian jazz pianist.
Artist: Sandra Dionisi
Art Directors: James Ireland and Barbara Solowan
Publication: Toronto Life

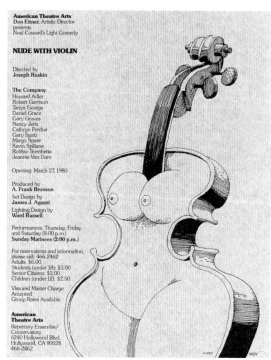

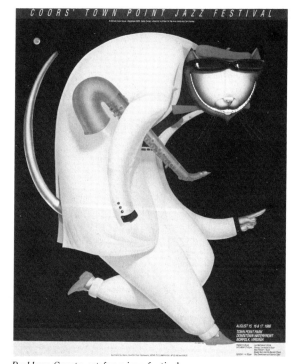

Problem: Design a small-format poster to advertise a production of the comedy
Nude with Violin.
Artist: Don Weller
Art Director: Don Weller
Client: American Theatre Arts Repertory

Problem: Create art for a jazz festival promotional poster.
Artist: Bill Mayer
Art Director: Nancy Walker
Client: Coors' Town Point Jazz Festival

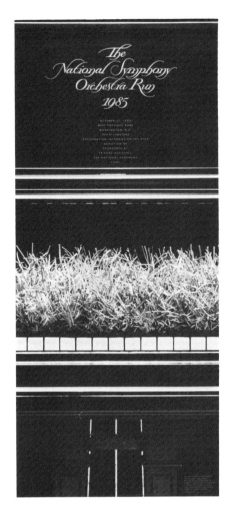

Problem: Design a logo for an American music studies institute.
Art Director: Michael Aron
Designer: Michael Aron
Client: Institute for Studies in American Music

Problem: Design a series of posters to promote an annual fund-raising marathon
Art Director: Kathleen Wilmes Herring
Designer: Kathleen Wilmes Herring
Client: The National Symphony Orchestra

Music

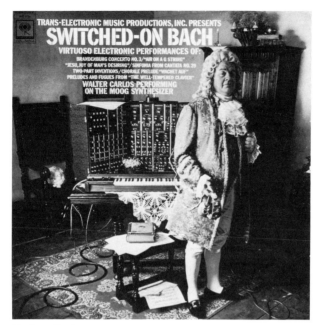

Problem: Design an album cover for a recording of synthesized versions of Bach works.
Photographer: Norman Griner
Art Director: John Berg
Designer: John Berg
Client: Columbia Records

Problem: Design an album cover for a collaborative record by two jazz artists.
Photographer: Arnold Rosenberg
Art Director: Paula Scher
Designer: Paula Scher
Client: CBS Records

Problem: Design an ad announcing corporate sponsorship of the arts.
Artist: Bill Mayer
Art Director: B. A. Albert
Client: Georgia Power

Problem: Design a promotional poster for the BYU Oratorio Choir.
Artist: McRay Magleby
Art Director: McRay Magleby
Client: Brigham Young University Oratorio Choir

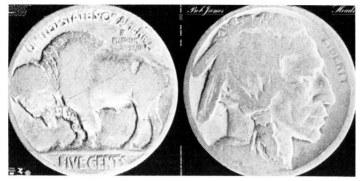

Problem: Design a jacket for an album entitled ''Heads.''
Photographer: John Paul Endress
Art Director: Paula Scher
Client: CBS Records

Problem: Design a promotional poster for an opera company.
Artists: Warren Wilkins and Tommer Peterson
Art Directors: Warren Wilkins and Tommer Peterson
Client: Seattle Opera Association

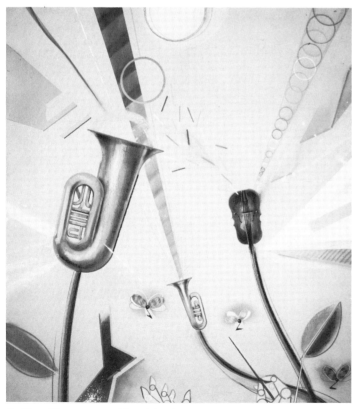

Problem: Illustrate an article celebrating the hundredth anniversary of the Boston Pops.
Artist: Andrzej Dudzinski
Art Director: Ronn Campisi
Publication: The Boston Globe

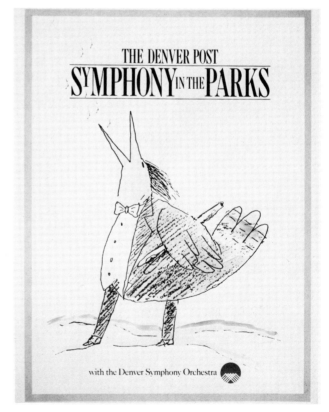

Problem: Create cover art for a guide to the Denver Symphony's summer schedule.
Artist: Bonnie Timmons
Art Director: Howard Klein
Publication: The Denver Post

Nature

Universe, Cosmos, Creation, Earth, Ecology, Habitat, Physical World, Flora and Fauna (See Animals, Environment)

As opposed to environmental subjects that connote a violation of the planet's resources, nature suggests an unencumbered representation of purity. The archetypal image is still Eden before the asp.

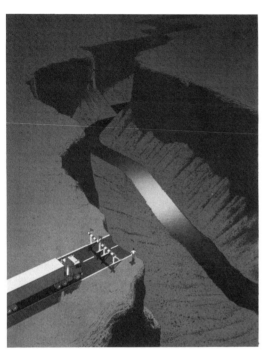

Problem: Unknown
Artist: Guy Billout
Art Director: Judy Garlan
Publication: The Atlantic

Problem: Design a poster announcing the AIGA spring events calendar.
Art Director: Kenneth Carbone
Designer: Allison Muench
Client: American Institute of Graphic Arts/New York

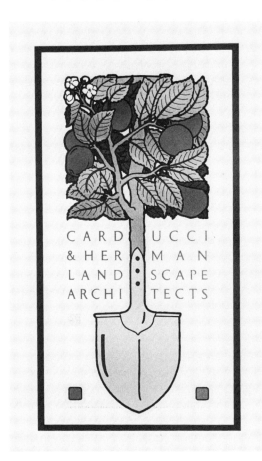

Problem: Design a logo for the Canyon Lakes real-estate development.
Artist: Michael Vanderbyl
Art Director: Michael Vanderbyl
Client: Brooks Resources, Harold Thompson Real Estate, Inc.

Problem: Design a logo for a firm that creates historically accurate landscape designs.
Artist: Jack Gernsheimer
Art Director: Jack Gernsheimer
Client: Historical Landscapes

Problem: Create a logo/symbol for a firm of landscape architects.
Artist: David Lance Goines
Art Director: David Lance Goines
Client: Carducci & Herman

Problem: Create art suitable for a catalog cover or a promotional mailer.
Artist: George Hardie
Art Director: George Hardie
Client: Winrow Nurseries

Parenthood

Father, Mother, Create, Nurture,
Raise, Sire, Family, Kin, Clan, Tribe
(See Birth, Celebration)

The family is sacred in most societies; therefore, parenthood is a highly charged subject. Though objectified "pictorial sign symbols" can be used to depict mother, father, sister, and brother, emotional representations are perhaps more appropriate.

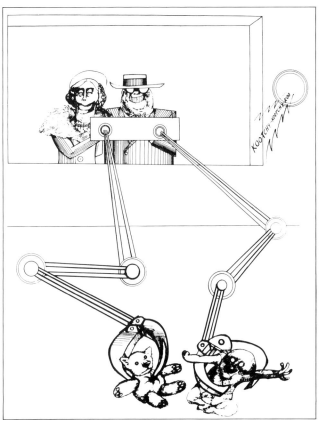

Problem: Depict "American parenting" for a book on contemporary American culture.
Artist: Ralph Steadman
Art Director: Bob Kingsbury
Client: Straight Arrow Press

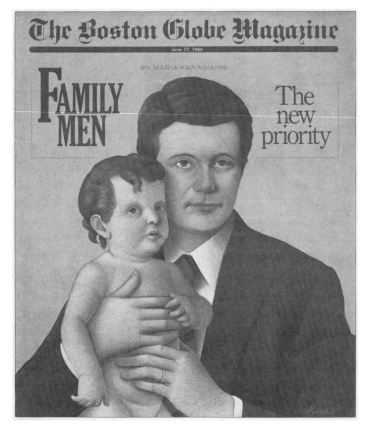

Problem: Illustrate a feature story on men and parenting.
Artist: Richard Mantel
Art Director: Ronn Campisi
Publication: The Boston Globe Magazine

M⊗THER

Problem: Design a logo for a magazine devoted to parenting.
Artist: Herb Lubalin
Art Director: Herb Lubalin
Publication: Mother & Child (never produced)

Artificial Insemination: Delivering Hope Where There Had Been Despair

Problem: Create magazine cover art for a feature story on artificial insemination.
Artist: Dugald Stermer
Art Director: Dugald Stermer
Publication: California Living

Problem: Design a logo for a parent advisory service.
Art Director: Dale K. Johnston
Designer: Dale K. Johnston
Client: American Guidance Services, Inc.

Problem: Create a logo design for a childcare placement service for the working parent.
Art Director: Dave Kottler
Designers: Dave Kottler and Paul Caldera
Client: MotherWorks, Inc.

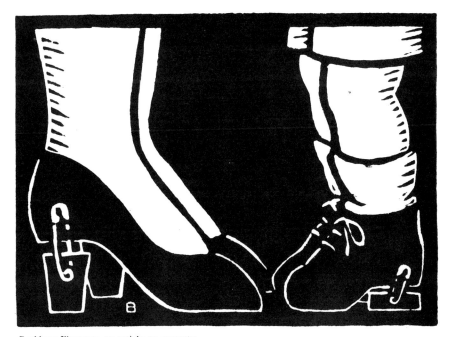

Problem: Illustrate an article on poverty among single mothers and the outlook for their children.
Artist: Bascove
Art Director: Patrick J. B. Flynn
Publication: The Progressive

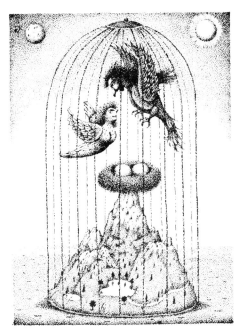

Problem: Create art for a book review.
Artist: Peter Sis
Art Director: Greg Ryan
Publication: The New York Times Book Review (illustration not used)

Peace

Nonviolent, Harmony, Quiet, Calm, Tranquillity, Accord (See Atomic, Bomb, Celebration, Human Relations, Power, War)

The dove, the lamb, and swords beaten into plowshares are biblical representations of the oldest human concern. By its nature, peace is harder to forcefully represent than warfare, but it is no less necessary.

Problem: Design a poster advocating peace.
Artist: Randall Enos
Art Director: Randall Enos
Client: The Shoshin Society

Problem: Design a fund-raising poster for a nuclear disarmament concert and rally.
Artist: Theo Dimson
Art Director: Theo Dimson
Client: Performing Artists for Nuclear Disarmament

Problem: Design a poster for a fund-raising dance marathon, ''Give Peace a Dance.''
Artist: Art Chantry
Art Director: Art Chantry
Client: Liz Smith and Give Peace a Dance

Problem: Illustrate an article on computers and world peace through communication and exchange of data.
Artist: Barbara Nessim
Art Director: Ronn Campisi
Publication: The Boston Globe Magazine

Problem: Design a poster
commemorating forty years of nuclear
peace.
Artist: McRay Magleby
Art Director: McRay Magleby
Client: The Shoshin Society

Problem: Design a poster promoting
peace efforts.
Artist: Bob Salpeter
Art Director: Bob Salpeter
Client: The Shoshin Society

Problem: Illustrate an article on
economic conversion—from military to
peaceful industrial production.
Artist: David Suter
Art Director: Patrick J. B. Flynn
Publication: The Progressive

Peace

Problem: Design a poster communicating the complete devastation inherent in a nuclear confrontation.
Artist: Rafal Olbinski
Art Director: Rafal Olbinski
Client: The Shoshin Society

Problem: Unknown
Artist: Tadahiko Ogawa
Art Director: Tadahiko Ogawa
Client: Unknown

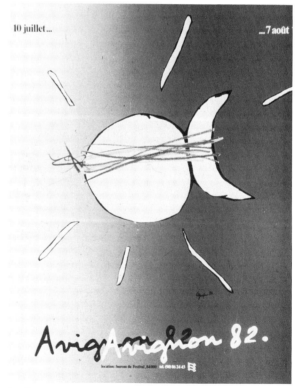

Problem: Design a poster advocating peace.
Artist: Lanny Sommese
Art Director: Lanny Sommese
Client: The Shoshin Society

Problem: Design a promotional poster for the Festival d'Avignon.
Artist: Alex Jordan
Art Director: Alex Jordan
Client: Festival d'Avignon

Problem Design a poster commemorating forty years of nuclear peace since the bombing of Hiroshima.
Art Director: Chris Hill
Designer: Jeff McKay
Client: The Shoshin Society

Problem: Design a poster promoting world peace.
Artist: Yoshio Akimoto
Art Director: Yoshio Akimoto
Client: Japan Graphic Designers Association

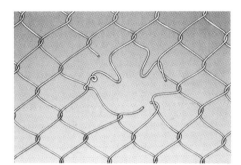

Problem: Create a simple, graphic image of peace for a postcard.
Artist: U. G. Sato
Art Director: U. G. Sato
Client: het Kaartenhuis, Amsterdam

Problem: Illustrate an editorial on the state of nuclear awareness and the peace movement.
Artist: R. O. Blechman
Art Director: J. C. Suares
Publication: The New York Times

Problem: Design a poster advocating peace.
Photographer: Hiroshi Koiwai
Artist: Masuteru Aoba
Art Director: Masuteru Aoba
Designers: Kenny Lui Kam-Yuen and Yoshiaki Otake
Client: A&A

Politics

Over time, the trademarks of partisan politics, such as Thomas Nast's Democratic donkey and Republican elephant, have become indelible, while the perception of politics is a more elusive problem to visualize.

Problem: Illustrate an article on problematic communications among White House departments and staff, and the tarnished image presented to the public by White House spokespersons.
Artist: Eugene Mihaesco
Art Director: Robert Best
Publication: New York

Problem: Illustrate an article on the vote.
Artist: Philippe Weisbecker
Art Director: David Harris
Publication: D Magazine

Problem: Illustrate an article on the bureaucratic problems facing farmers who are foreclosed.
Artist: Henrik Drescher
Art Director: Patrick J. B. Flynn
Publication: The Progressive

Problem: Illustrate an article entitled "The Known World," a reordering of countries of world importance based on media coverage.
Artist: Ron Hauge
Art Director: Wes Anderson
Publication: The Village Voice

Problem: Create magazine cover art for a story on today's KGB.
Artist: James Marsh
Art Director: Nigel Holmes
Publication: Time

Problem: Illustrate a Sunday news magazine feature on Cleveland's leftist faction.
Artist: Mark Andresen
Art Director: Greg Paul
Publication: The Plain Dealer Sunday Magazine

Politics

Problem: Illustrate an article entitled "The Gnomes of Bilderberg."
Artist: Don Ivan Punchatz
Art Director: Joe Brooks
Publication: Penthouse

Problem: Create cover art for a magazine feature story on the state of the Republican party, and its image among voters, after the Reagan presidency.
Artist: Randall Enos
Art Director: Patrick J. B. Flynn
Publication: The Progressive

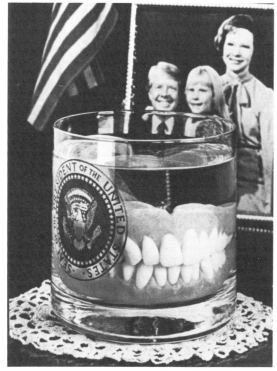

Problem: Illustrate a satirical article on the image of the First Family during the Carter Administration.
Artist: Gordon Mortensen
Art Director: Gordon Mortensen
Publication: Skeptic

Problem: Create a poster image to encourage employees to become involved in the legislative process.
Art Director/Designer: Melanie Roher
Client: Mobil Oil Corporation

Power

Could power be the real root of all evil? The familiar symbols of power are usually charged icons, like the swastika, but the *idea* of strength can also be depicted in more subtle ways.

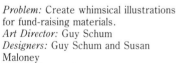

FUNDOWSKI
RAISES BIG
LETTUCE FAST

THE GREAT
PROFUNDO'S SEMINARS
RAISE NO
SMALL POTATOES

Problem: Create whimsical illustrations for fund-raising materials.
Art Director: Guy Schum
Designers: Guy Schum and Susan Maloney
Client: Council for the Advancement and Support of Education

Problem: Illustrate an article on strength and fitness.
Artist: Lou Beach
Art Director: Lloyd Ziff
Publication: New West

117

Race, Racism

Sectarianism, Prejudice, Bigotry, Apartheid, Ethnocentricity, Discrimination, Cultural Bias (See Human Relations, Politics)

Ethnicity portrayed in graphic art has long been criticized for promoting racism because the process of picture making involves standardizations that often result in simplistic stereotypes.

Problem: Illustrate an article on the friction between Congress and the Reagan Administration as to standards for granting political asylum.
Artist: Bob Gale
Art Director: Rhoda Gubernick
Publication: The Atlantic

Problem: Illustrate an article on the recent increase in activity among members of the Ku Klux Klan.
Artist: Bonnie Timmons
Art Director: Randy Miller
Publication: The Denver Post

Problem: Create magazine cover art for a feature story on the resurgence of bigotry in California.
Artist: Michael Schwab
Art Director: Laura Lamar
Publication: Focus (the magazine of PBS station KQED, San Francisco)

Problem: Illustrate an article on Soviet oppression as enforced by Andropov's KGB.
Artist: Bonnie Timmons
Art Director: Bonnie Timmons
Publication: The Denver Post

Real Estate

Land, Property, Realty, Development, Urban, Suburban, Rural (See Economy, Environment)

Land is a most profitable commodity. Its sale and development are the basis of countless newspaper and magazine articles and advertising brochures, and it is therefore one of the most overexposed themes of modern times.

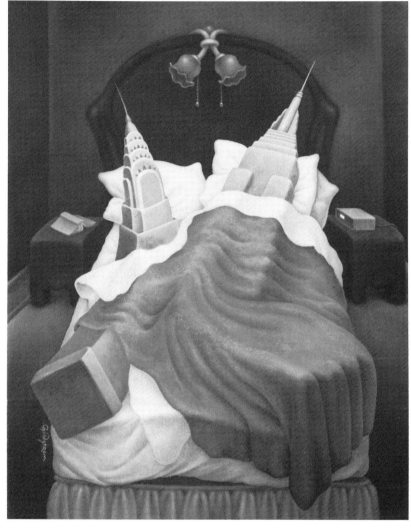

Problem: Create a logo for a real-estate development firm.
Artist: Gregory Cutshaw
Art Director: Gregory Cutshaw
Client: Eagle Ridge Development Company

Problem: Illustrate the incestuous nature of the New York real-estate market.
Artist: Bob Goldstrom
Art Director: Unknown
Client: Unknown

Problem: Create art for a corporate ad expressing concern, and hope, for the future of America's cities.
Artist: René Magritte
Art Director/Designer: James Miho
Client: Atlantic Richfield Corporation

Real Estate

Problem: Create poster and brochure art for material promoting a design conference in Park City, Utah.
Art Director/Designer: Don Weller
Client: TDCTJHTBIPC (The Design Conference That Just Happens To Be In Park City)

Problem: Create a poster celebrating completion of the tallest building in Tampa, Florida.
Artist: George Tscherny
Art Director: George Tscherny
Client: Samuel C. Florman

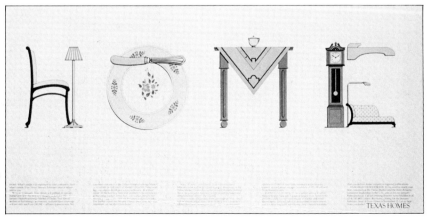

Problem: Create a poster announcing the opening of a home interiors show.
Art Director/Designer: Cap Pannell
Client: Texas Homes

Religion

Faith, Creed, Church, Beliefs, Cult, Denomination, Orthodoxy, Theology, Evangelism, Gospel

No other book eclipses the Bible as a source of visual imagery. Most representations of good and evil are derived from its distinctive metaphors. Visual critiques of religion also draw from this wellspring of inspiration.

Problem: Design and illustrate registration materials for a symposium on comparative world religions.
Artist: McRay Magleby
Art Director: McRay Magleby
Client: Brigham Young University

Problem: Illustrate an article on lesbian nuns.
Artist: Cathy Hull
Art Director: Joe McNeill
Publication: Penthouse

Problem: Create art to accompany a review of the book *Mephistopheles: The Devil in the Modern World.*
Artist: Jose Cruz
Art Director: Rhoda Gubernick
Publication: The Atlantic

Religion

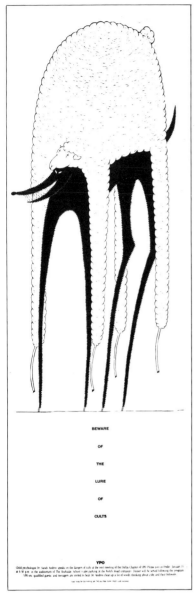

BEWARE

OF

THE

LURE

OF

CULTS

YPO

Problem: Create poster art for a
speakers' evening on the danger of cults.
Artist: Chris Rovillo
Art Director: Chris Rovillo
Client: Young Presidents Organization,
Dallas Chapter

Problem: Illustrate an editorial/article on
religion and deception.
Artist: Hans Georg Rauch
Art Director: Unknown
Client: Unknown

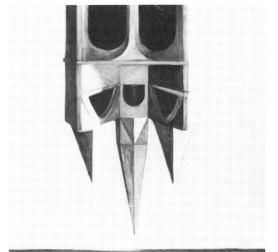

Problem: Create a graphic commentary
on the power of the church in America,
and the potential result of that power's
misuse.
Artist: David Ayriss
Art Director: David Ayriss
Client: Self-promotion

Problem: Create an illustration for an
article on right-wing religious movements
and peace politics.
Artist: Randall Enos
Art Director: Victor Navasky
Publication: The Nation

Science

Experimentation, Biology, Chemistry, Physics (See Atomic, Intelligence, Technology)

Science is rich in visuals, deriving its symbols from the most simple tool (a test tube) to the most complex machinery. And since science is in constant flux, so are the conceptual images associated with it.

Problem: Illustrate an article on evolution.
Artist: Catherine Denvir
Art Director: Chris Jones
Publication: New Scientist

Problem: Illustrate a book excerpt on the legacy of ape languages.
Artist: Charles B. Slackman
Art Director: Judy Garlan
Designer: Rhoda Gubernick
Publication: The Atlantic

Services

Service, which includes the day-to-day requirements of an industrial society, provides a miscellany of recurring problems in design. How does one represent construction, plumbing, and garbage pickup as not simply mechanical concerns?

Problem: Design a logo for a plumber.
Art Director/Designer: Steve Grigg
Client: Speirs Plumbing

Problem: Design a logo for a painting contractor.
Art Director/Designer: D. C. Stipp
Client: Willis Painting Contractors

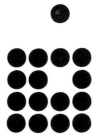

Problem: Design a logo for a professional placement service.
Art Director/Designer: Bonnie Segal
Client: Stephen Adler Associates, Inc.

Problem: Create a logo and stationery system for an architectural firm.
Art Director/Designer: Sue T. Crolick
Client: Thacher & Thompson, Architects

Problem: Design a logo for two building contractors.
Art Director/Designer: Don Faia
Client: Peeples Brothers Construction Company

Problem: Design a logo for a residential painting contractor.
Art Director/Designer: Ken Hegstrom
Client: Final Touch Painting

Problem: Design a logo for a woodworking craftsperson
Art Director/Designer: Luis D. Acevedo
Client: McKinzie Milling and Manufacturing

Sex

Eroticism, Sensualism, Libido, Passion, Gender, Carnality, Mating

As allusion, metaphor, and allegory, sex has underscored many graphic images throughout history, from the depiction of the sex act to the difference between the sexes to the employment of sex as a tool of power.

Problem: Illustrate an article entitled "Kazmar's Burden."
Artist: Dennis Noble
Art Director: Ken Rodmell
Publication: Toronto Life

Problem: Create editorial illustration for an article on women and multiple sex partners.
Artist: Blair Drawson
Art Director: Tom Staebler
Publication: Playboy

Problem: Create paperback art for a book by Georges Simenon.
Artist: Bascove
Art Director: Harris Lewine
Client: Harcourt Brace Jovanovich

Sex

Problem: Create editorial art for a
satirical commentary on the problems of
Jim and Tammy Bakker.
Artist: Anita Kunz
Art Director: Fred Woodward
Publication: Regardie's

Problem: Illustrate an article on the
effects of clandestine love relationships
among co-workers.
Artist: Jerzy Kolacz
Art Director: Steve Manley
Publication: Canadian Business

Problem: Create album jacket art for a
record entitled ''Multiplication.''
Artist: David Wilcox
Art Director: Paula Scher
Client: CBS Records

Problem: Illustrate an article on transsexuals.
Artist: Dagmar Frinta
Art Director: Greg Paul
Publication: The Plain Dealer

Problem: Create art for the fall preview issue of *New York* magazine.
Artist: Seymour Chwast
Art Director: Walter Bernard
Publication: New York

Problem: Design a logo for a ranch which sells vials of semen from star bulls for artificial insemination.
Art Director: Steven Sessions
Designer: Steven Sessions
Client: Star Semen, Inc.

Sports

Every game has a distinctive vocabulary of recognizable images. The need to invent new ones is necessary only with the invention of new sports. Overcoming the traditional uses of recognizable images is the designer's challenge.

Problem: Create a promotional poster for an annual event for windsurfers and sail enthusiasts.
Artist: Craig Dicken
Designer: Craig Dicken
Client: Sailworks, a marine supply retail establishment.

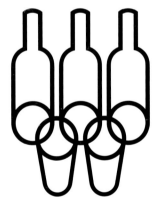

Problem: Design a logo for a restaurant/bar's special promotion, the "Bartender Olympics."
Art Director/Designer: Kenny Garrison
Client: T.G.I. Friday's, Inc.

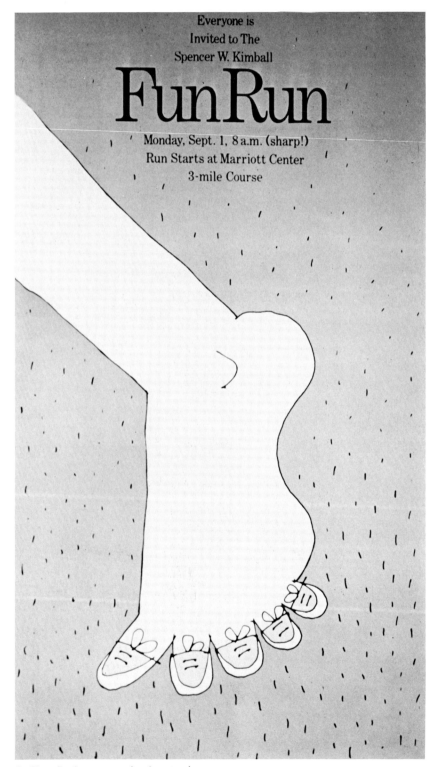

Problem: Design a promotional poster for a university-sponsored running event.
Artist: McRay Magleby
Art Director/Designer: McRay Magleby
Client: Brigham Young University

Problem: Design a logo for the Moscow Olympic Games.
Art Director/Designer: Félix Beltrán
Client: Ministerio de Cultura, Havana

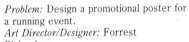

Problem: Design a promotional poster for a running event.
Art Director/Designer: Forrest Richardson
Client: The Phoenix Marathon

Problem: Illustrate an article on boxing.
Artist: George Snow
Art Director: George Snow
Publication: Unpublished

Sports

Problem: Create cover art for a Sunday magazine feature article.
Artist: Elwood H. Smith
Art Director: Michael Walsh
Publication: The Washington Post Magazine

Problem: Create art for a sports feature article.
Artist: Paul Meisel
Art Director: Andrea DuRif
Publication: Racquet Quarterly

Problem: Design a logo for a swim school.
Art Director/Designer: Harry Murphy
Client: Marin Swim School

Problem: Design a logo/mark for a racquet club.
Art Director/Designer: Steven Sessions
Client: The Racquet Club, Detroit

Problem: Create cover art for a magazine feature on baseball trivia.
Artist: John Craig
Art Director: Greg Paul
Publication: Sunshine (reprinted for *Pacific*)

Problem: Design a logo for a volleyball team.
Artist: Jeff Kimble
Art Director/Designer: Jeff Kimble
Client: Animals Volleyball Team

Problem: Illustrate an article on sports medicine.
Artist: Stuart Goldenberg
Art Director: Mike Valenti
Publication: The New York Times

Technology

Industry, Commerce, Engineering, Knowledge, Tools (See Computers, Industry, Intelligence, and Science)

Rube Goldberg is the master of industrial symbology. Who has better humanized the contraptions of high-tech society? Many of these inventions are so beyond average comprehension that humor proves to be the best leveller.

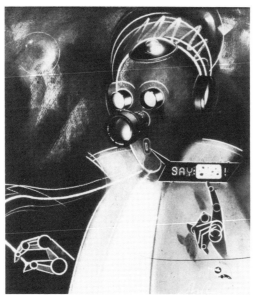

Problem: Create cover art for a newspaper special section on cameras.
Artist: Andrzej Dudzinski
Art Director: Miriam Smith
Publication: Newsday

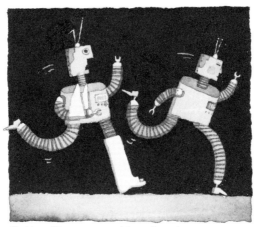

Problem: Illustrate an article on how the United States is losing the robot race with Japan.
Artist: John Segal
Art Director: Mike Todd
Publication: The New York Times

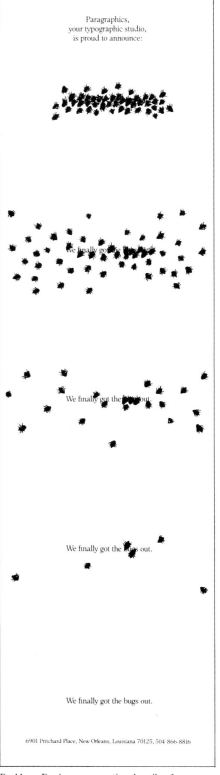

Problem: Design a promotional mailer for a newly opened typography shop.
Art Director/Designer: Tom Varisco
Client: Paragraphics, Inc.

Problem: Design a logo for Southwestern Cable System.
Art Director: Kelly Davenport
Designer: Leonard Walker Torres
Client: Southwestern Cable

Problem: Create cover art for a Sunday magazine feature article on the boom in toy robot sales.
Artist: Lou Brooks
Art Director: Lynn Staley
Publication: The Boston Globe Magazine

Problem: Illustrate an article on the myths/truths in the perception of Japanese technological superiority.
Artist: Christopher Bing
Art Director: Nancy Cahners
Designer: Kathleen Sayre
Publication: M.I.T. Technology Review

Technology

Problem: Illustrate an article entitled
"Why Things Don't Work."
Artist: Sandra Hendler
Art Director: Arthur Paul
Designer: Skip Williamson
Publication: Playboy

Problem: Illustrate a review of a book of
tips from successful CEOs.
Artist: Mirko Ilic
Art Director: Steven Heller
*Publication: The New York Times Book
Review*

ECLIPSE

Problem: Design a logo for a new line of reflective glass.
Art Director/Designer: Jeff Kimble
Client: Libbey-Owens-Ford Co.

POWERED**FLIGHT**DAY

December 17, 1983
Bradley Air Museum

This poster courtesy of Pratt & Whitney,
a division of United Technologies

Problem: Create a logo and stationery for a structural engineer.
Artist: Ian McIlroy
Art Director/Designer: Ian McIlroy
Client: Jim McColl Associates

Problem: Design a cover for a promotional brochure for *Powered Flight Day.*
Artist: Robert Appleton
Art Director/Designer: Robert Appleton
Client: Pratt & Whitney Aircraft

Theatre

"All the world is a stage" is the verbal equivalent of the most common visual clichés. However, as with all venerable themes, recurrent images have a usefulness, and classic theatrical symbols can be freshly reapplied.

Problem: Design a promotional poster for a performance of *Othello*.
Photographers: Michael van de Sand and Gunther Rambow
Art Director/Designer: Gunther Rambow
Client: Unknown

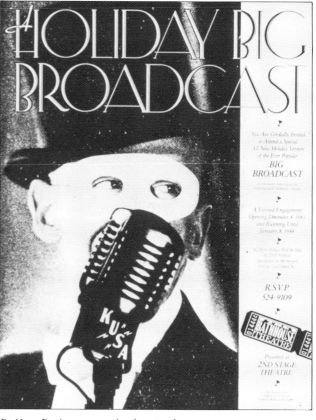

Problem: Design a promotional poster for a cultural event.
Artist: Art Chantry
Art Director/Designer: Art Chantry
Client: The Bathhouse Theater

Problem: Design a logo for a playwright.
Art Director/Designer: Suzanne Redding
Client: Toni Press

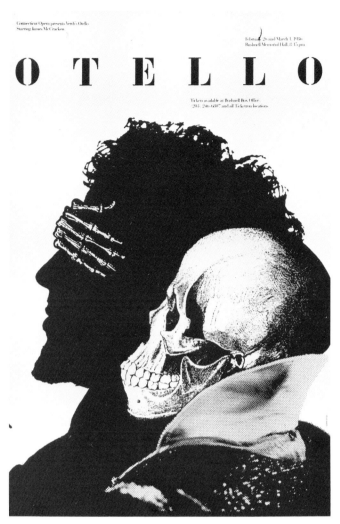

Connecticut Opera presents Verdi's Otello.
Starring James McCracken

February 26 and March 1, 1986
Bushnell Memorial Hall, 8:15 pm

O T E L L O

Tickets available at Bushnell Box Office,
203-246-6807 and all Ticketron locations.

Problem: Design a poster for a
performance of Verdi's *Otello*.
Art Director/Designer: Robert Appleton
Client: The Connecticut Opera

HVIDOVRE
TEATER

Problem: Create a poster promoting a
theatre company.
Artist: Per Arnoldi
Art Director: Per Arnoldi
Client: Hvidovre Theatre Company

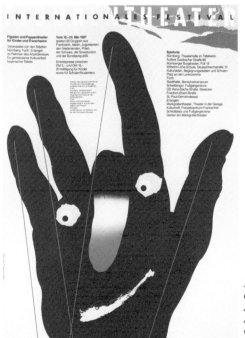

Problem: Design a poster for a series of
cultural events.
Artist: Alan Le Quernec
Art Director: Alan Le Quernec
Client: The City of Nuremburg, West
Germany

Theatre

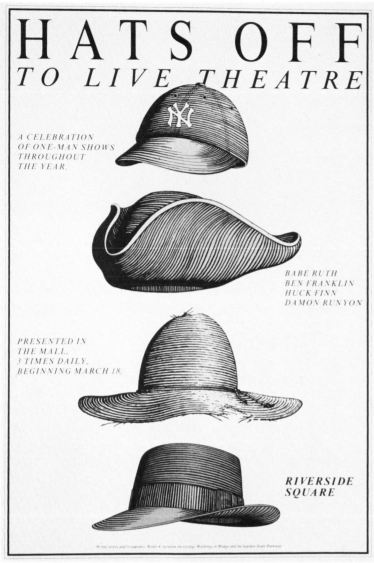

Problem: Design a poster announcing a series of theatrical monologues sponsored by a department store.
Artist: Cap Pannell
Art Director/Designer: Cap Pannell
Client: JMB/Federated Department Stores

Problem: Design a promotional poster for a performance of *The Merry Widow.*
Art Director/Designer: Robert Appleton
Client: The Connecticut Opera

Problem: Design a logo for a performing arts service.
Artists: Betty Barsamian, Karen Fenlon
Art Director/Designer: Michael Manwaring
Client: Performing Arts Services, Inc.

Time

Duration, Date, Day, Week, Hour, Minute, Life, Future, Present, Past, Chronology, Infinity, Genesis (See Aging, Death)

The sundial was perhaps the first of a series of time-related symbols that have apparently ended for now with the letterforms of the digital clock. Yet the unorthodox depictions of time are as numerous as time is elusive.

Problem: Design a calendar as a promotional piece for a printer.
Art Director/Designer: Kathleen Wilmes Herring
Client: Westland Printers

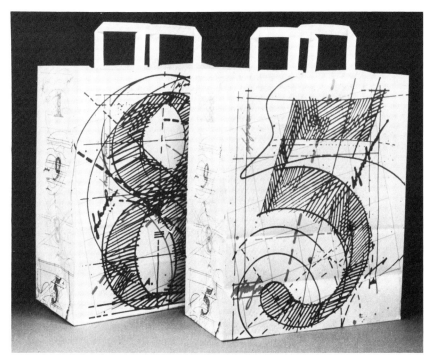

Problem: Design a New Year's holiday shopping bag for Bloomingdale's.
Art Director/Designer: Tim Girvin
Client: Bloomingdale's

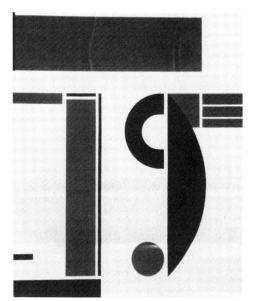
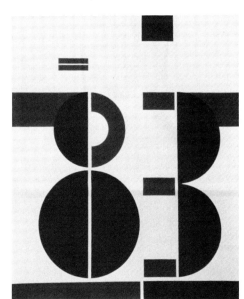

Problem: Design a New Year's holiday shopping bag for Bloomingdale's.
Art Director: J. Richard Hsu
Designer: Melanie Marder Parks
Client: Bloomingdale's

Time

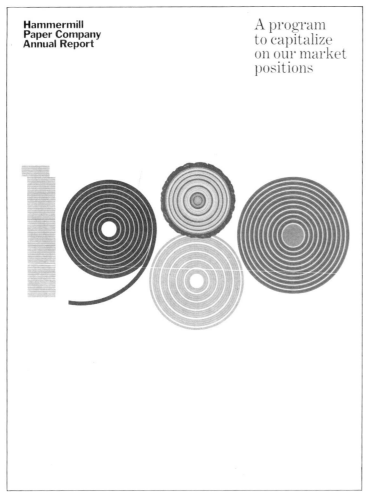

Problem: Create cover art for a forest products company annual report.
Art Director/Designer: Peter Good
Client: Hammermill Paper Company

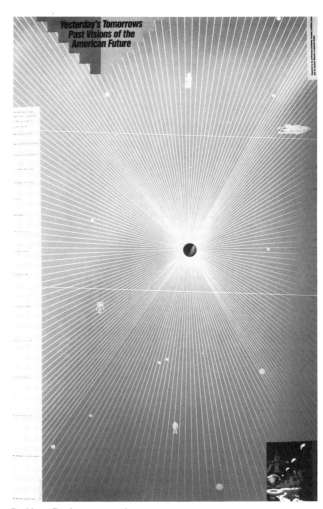

Problem: Design a cover for a promotional poster.
Art Director/Designer: James Miho
Client: Champion International

Problem: Create art for a corporate promotional brochure.
Artist: Richard Mantel
Art Director/Designer: Wes Keebler
Client: Reinsurance Facilities Corporation

Transport

Vehicle, Carriage, Car, Plane, Bus, Ship (See Industry, Technology)

Some of the most graphically sophisticated machinery are old cars, boats, planes, and trains. Though once designed to emphasize their machine parts and functions, they are now the playthings of style-conscious designers.

Problem: Create editorial art for an article entitled "Heaven On Wheels," about driving as a "religious experience."
Artist: Tom Curry
Art Director: Fred Woodward
Publication: Texas Monthly

Problem: Design a poster for an exhibition of British airport design.
Art Directors/Designers: Marcello Minale and Brian Tattersfield
Client: British Airports Authority

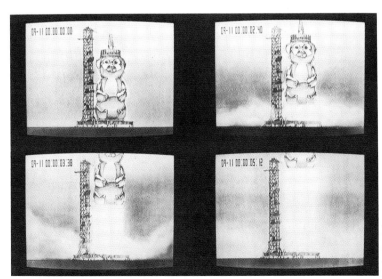

Problem: Create art for a calendar on the theme of flight for a firm specializing in airport architecture.
Art Director/Designer: David Ayriss
Client: W. Haas Associates

Transport

Problem: Create a logo for a charter seaplane service.
Art Director/Designer: Woody Pirtle
Client: Sea Wings

Problem: Design a trademark to identify government-sanctioned taxi services.
Art Director/Designer: Félix Beltrán
Client: Ministerio de Transporte, Havana

Problem: Design a logo for the International Customized Motorcycle Awards Exhibition.
Art Director/Designer: Steven Sessions
Client: International Customized Motorcycle Awards Exhibition, Atlanta

Problem: Create cover art for a magazine.
Artist/Art Director: Rudy VanderLans
Publication: Emigré

Travel

Vacation, Tourism, Migration, Voyage, Journey, Quest (See Transport)

Cars, planes, trains, and so on, are merely the conveyances for travel. This theme not only includes the journey, but the act of discovery. With travel as a major aspect of "lifestyle," images of its phases are in demand.

Problem: Design a promotional postcard for a travel service.
Artist: Philippe Weisbecker
Art Director: Holly Russell, Altman & Manley
Client: ABC International

Problem: Illustrate an article on Woody Herman and his band, the Thundering Herd.
Artist: Peter Sis
Art Director: Rhoda Gubernick
Publication: The Atlantic

Travel

Problem: Design a mark for a travel agency.
Art Director/Designer: D. Bruce Zahor
Client: Command Travel, Inc.

Problem: Design a mark for an international cruise line.
Art Director/Designer: U. G. Sato
Client: Cruise International, Inc.

Starting today, you can fly from Tel Aviv to Cairo. On El Al.

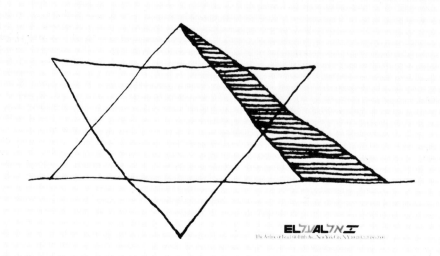

Problem: Design ad art for an airline.
Art Director: Unknown
Designer: Joan Niborg
Client: El Al Airlines

Destination

Problem: Design a masthead logo for an in-flight magazine.
Art Directors: Philip Waugh and Arthur Eisenberg
Designer: Philip Waugh
Client: Braniff/Brighton Square Publishing

Violence

Fury, Rage, Crime, Brute Force, Commotion, Riot, Anarchy, Revolution (See Bomb, Crime, Death, Human Relations, Peace, Race, War)

How to represent physical hatred without gore is a difficult problem. Certain clues, such as a pained expression, a rigor-mortised hand, or a drop of blood serve the purpose but do not really solve the problem.

Problem: Illustrate an article on violence begetting violence.
Artist: Renée Klein
Art Director: Ronn Campisi
Publication: The Boston Globe Sunday Magazine

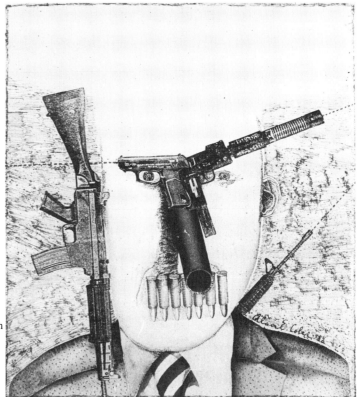

Problem: Illustrate an article on suburban professionals outfitting themselves with heavy firearms.
Artist: Alan E. Cober
Art Director: Don Owens
Publication: Dallas Times Herald, Westward magazine

Violence

Problem: Illustrate the concepts of
accident and blame.
Artist: Shigeo Fukuda
Art Director: Shigeo Fukuda
Client: Shigeo Fukuda, Green Collections
Gallery show

Problem: Illustrate an anti–gun control
editorial article.
Artist: Bob Gale
Art Director: Jerelle Kraus
Publication: The New York Times

146

Problem: Design and illustrate a
corporate ad supporting individuality and
questioning of authority.
Art Director/Designer: James Miho
Client: Container Corporation of America

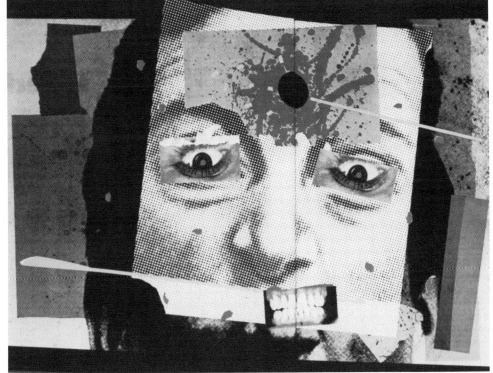

Problem: Create editorial art for a short
story entitled ''The Gunshot.''
Artist: Lou Beach
Art Director: Roger Carpenter
Publication: Oui

War

Conflict, Battle, Clash, Hostility, Bloodshed, Aggression, Militarism, Dominance, Defense (See Atomic, Bomb, Death, Human Relations, Peace, Politics, Power, Race, Violence)

For this regrettably recurrent theme, artists have exhausted the timeworn, yet decidedly effective, images, while replenishing the arsenal with newer weapons that have become more streamlined and less graphic over time.

Problem: Create magazine cover art illustrating (and commenting on) arms control.
Artist: Mick Haggerty
Art Director: Lloyd Ziff
Publication: Vanity Fair

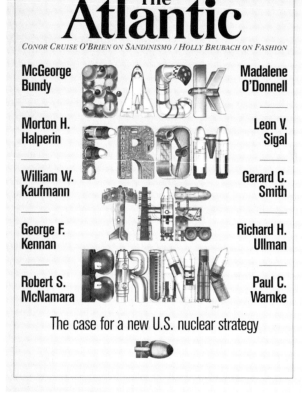

Problem: Create magazine cover art for a feature on nuclear disarmament talks.
Artist: Jozef Sumichrast
Art Director: Judy Garlan
Publication: The Atlantic

Problem: Illustrate an article on the U.S. provision of arms and aid to the Nicaraguan *contras.*
Artist: Lane Smith
Art Director: Patrick J. B. Flynn
Publication: The Progressive

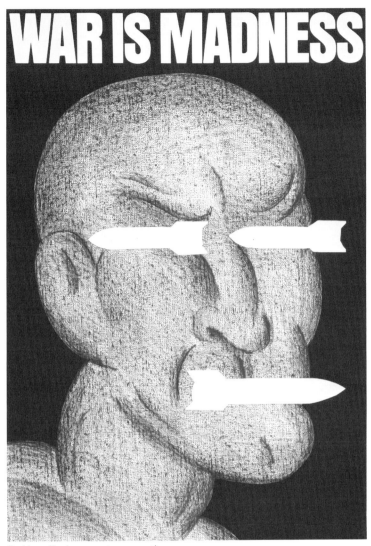

WAR IS MADNESS

Problem: Design a poster promoting
world peace.
Artist: Seymour Chwast
Art Director/Designer: Seymour Chwast
Client: The Shoshin Society

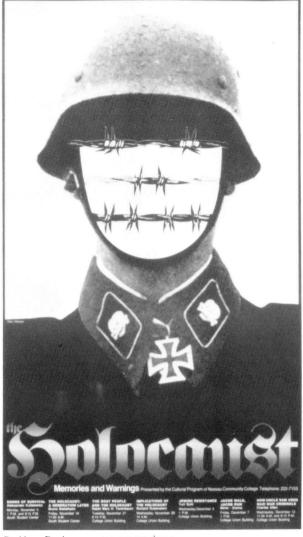

Problem: Design a poster announcing a
series of lectures on the Holocaust.
Artist: Gary Viskupic
Art Director/Designer: Gary Viskupic
Client: Nassau Community College

Problem: Illustrate an article on the
possession of nuclear weapons and the
potential for disaster.
Artist: Brad Holland
Art Director: Jerelle Kraus
Publication: The New York Times

War

Problem: Create magazine cover art for a feature on military experts and how they have formulated our "nuclear defense plan."
Artist: Marshall Arisman
Art Director: Ronn Campisi
Publication: The Boston Globe Magazine

Problem: Illustrate an article on the "New Right" in American politics and its neo-conservative stance.
Artist: John Craig
Art Director: Theo Kouvatsos
Publication: Playboy

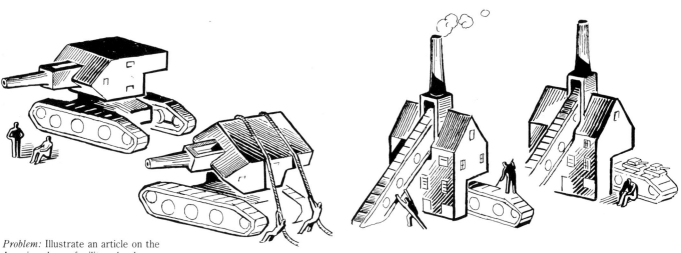

Problem: Illustrate an article on the American love of military hardware.
Artist: David Suter
Art Director: Patrick J. B. Flynn
Publication: The Progressive.

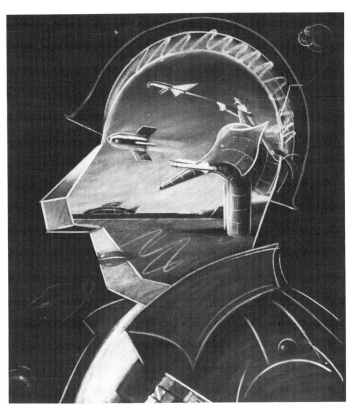

Problem: Illustrate an article analyzing
the power of the military.
Artist: Andrzej Dudzinski
Art Director: Ronn Campisi
Publication: The Boston Globe

Problem: Illustrate an article on arms
dealers.
Artist: Eugene Mihaesco
Art Director: Eric Seidman
Publication: The New York Times

Problem: Illustrate an article on the rift
in civil relations among Salvadorans due
to the war.
Artist: Bascove
Art Director: Patrick J. B. Flynn
Publication: The Progressive

War

Problem: Illustrate an editorial on conscientious objectors and the draft.
Artist: Bob Gale
Art Director: Jerelle Kraus
Publication: The New York Times

Problem: Illustrate an article on the newly organized, and powerful, liberal ''Green'' political movement in Germany.
Artist: Henrik Drescher
Art Director: Patrick J. B. Flynn
Publication: The Progressive

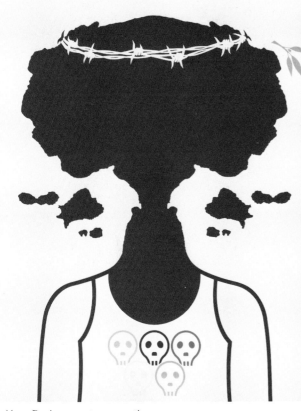

核戦争に勝利者はない。
There is No Victor in Nuclear War.

核兵器廃絶
Against Nuclear Weapons

WAR WASTE ENERGY

戦争はエネルギーの無駄使い

Problem: Design a poster promoting
nuclear peace.
Art Director/Designer: Hirokatsu Hijikata
Client: Peace Foundation

Problem: Design a poster promoting peace.
Artist: Masuteru Aoba
Art Director/Designer: Masuteru Aoba
Client: Unknown

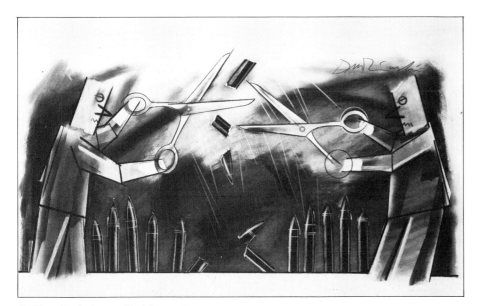

Problem: Illustrate an editorial on nuclear
disarmament.
Artist: Andrzej Dudzinski
Art Director: Jerelle Kraus
Publication: The New York Times

Artists Index

Artists Index

Art Directors/Designers Index

Art Directors/Designers Index